the
Best
Little Book Club
in Town

NAOMI ALDERMAN lives in London. She won the 2006 Orange Award for New Writers with her controversial debut novel, *Disobedience*. Her latest novel, *The Lessons*, about a group of Oxford students who discover that their time at university provides little grounding for what life will throw at them, is out now.

ELIZABETH BUCHAN lives in London with her husband and has two children. She worked in publishing before becoming a full-time author in 1985. She has written eleven novels, including *Consider the Lily*, which won the Romantic Novelists' Association Novel of the Year Award in 1994, and *Revenge of the Middle-Aged Woman*, which was made into a televised drama for CBS in 2004 and was a *Sunday Times* and *New York Times* bestseller. Her latest novel, *Separate Beds*, a timely story of recession, family and love, is out now.

TESS CALLAHAN's debut novel, *April and Oliver*, explores what happens when the last person you want in your life is the only one who can save it. It is out now. She has written for *The New York Times Magazine*, National Public Radio, *Agni*, and other literary magazines. A teacher, painter and mother of twins, she lives and writes in New Jersey.

MAVIS CHEEK was born and grew up in Wimbledon. She began her working life at Editions Alecto, the contemporary art publishers. She then attended Hillcroft College for Women from where she graduated in Arts with distinction. After her daughter Bella was born, she began her writing career in earnest; journalism and travel writing at first, then short stories, and eventually, in 1988, her novel *Pause between Acts* was published by Bodley Head and it won the *She*/John Menzies First Novel Prize. She is the author of fifteen novels including *Mrs Fytton's Country Life*, *Janice Gentle Gets Sexy*, *Truth to Tell* and, most recently, *The Lovers of Pound Hill*. She now lives and writes in Wiltshire.

TRACY CHEVALIER grew up in Washington, DC. She moved to England at the age of twenty-two and worked for several years as a reference book editor. In 1994, she graduated from the University of East Anglia with an MA in Creative Writing. Her second novel, *Girl with a Pearl Earring*, was an international bestseller and won the Barnes and Nobel Discover award. It was adapted into an Oscar-nominated film starring Colin Firth and Scarlett Johansson and a West End stage production. Her subsequent novels have all met with critical acclaim and commercial success. She lives in London with her husband and son.

LEE CHILD was born in 1954 in Coventry, but spent his formative years in Birmingham. After law school and part-time work in the theatre he joined Granada Television for what turned out to be an eighteen-year career as a presentation director. During his tenure his company made *Brideshead Revisited*, *The Jewel in the Crown*, *Prime Suspect* and *Cracker*. He was fired in 1995 at the age of forty as a result of corporate restructuring so, always a voracious reader, he sat down to write a book, *Killing Floor*. It was an immediate success and launched the Jack Reacher series which has grown in sales and impact with every new instalment. Lee divides his time between the US and France.

HELEN DUNMORE is a novelist, poet, short story and children's writer. Among other awards her work has received the Orange Prize for Fiction, the McKitterick Prize, the Nestlé Children's Book Prize Silver Medal and first prize in the National Poetry Competition. Her books have been translated into twenty-eight languages, and her latest novel is *The Betrayal*, published in paperback in 2011. She is a Fellow of the Royal Society of Literature.

JANE FALLON was born in north London the youngest of five children. Her first job was as a 'Girl Friday' in a small theatrical and literary agency. She went on to work as a script editor and then a producer, responsible for several hit shows including the award-winning drama series *This Life* and *Teachers*. One night in October 2004 when she couldn't sleep she came up with the idea for her first novel, *Getting Rid of Matthew*. At the same moment, she realised that she never wanted to make another TV show again. The book went on to become a *Sunday Times* bestseller as have the follow-ups *Got You Back* and *Foursome*. She has just completed her fourth novel.

KATIE FFORDE lives in Gloucestershire with her husband and some of her three children. Recently her old hobbies of ironing and housework have given way to singing, Flamenco dancing and husky racing. She claims this keeps her fit. She is the bestselling author of seventeen novels.

ESTHER FREUD was born in London in 1963. She trained as an actress before writing her first novel, *Hideous Kinky*, which was shortlisted for the John Llewellyn Rhys Prize and was made into a feature film starring Kate Winslet. Her other novels are *Peerless Flats*, *Summer at Gaglow*, *The Wild*, *The Sea House*, *Love Falls* and *Lucky Break*. In 1993 Esther Freud was chosen by Granta as one of the Best of Young British Novelists.

TESS GERRITSEN was a graduate of Stanford University and went on to medical school at the University of California, San Francisco, where she was awarded her M.D. While on maternity leave from her work as a physician, she began to write fiction and in 1987, her first novel, *Call After Midnight*, was published. Tess's first medical thriller, *Harvest*, was released in 1996, and it marked her debut on the *New York Times* bestseller list. A regular top five international bestseller, her books have been translated into thirty-seven languages, and more than twenty million copies have been sold around the world. Her most recent novel, *The Killing Place*, the latest in the highly popular Rizzoli and Isles Series, is out now.

DAISY GOODWIN is an author, the producer of BAFTA-winning TV programmes including *The Apprentice*, and founder of Silver River Productions. She has written an autobiography titled *Silver River*, as well as numerous poetry anthologies and a novel, *My Last Duchess*. Daisy is married and has two daughters.

SOPHIE HANNAH is an award-winning poet and author. Her novel *The Other Half Lives* was shortlisted for the 2010 Independent Booksellers' Book of the Year Award, while *The Point of Rescue* has been adapted for television. She started by writing poetry, publishing the first of five anthologies at the age of twenty-four, and her *Pessimism for Beginners* was nominated for the T.S. Eliot Prize for verse. It was at this point that Sophie turned to crime novels and she has now sold over half a million copies. Her sixth thriller, *Lasting Damage* is out now. Sophie lives with her husband and children in Cambridge.

RACHEL HEATH's first novel, *The Finest Type of English Womanhood*, was shortlisted for the 2009 Costa First Novel Award and the 2010 Authors' Club Best First Novel Award. She lives in Bath with her husband and three children.

WENDY HOLDEN began her career as a journalist, writing for the *Sunday Telegraph* magazine, the *Sunday Times* and the *Mail on Sunday*'s *You* magazine. She published her first novel, *Simply Divine*, in 1999 and has released nine other top ten bestsellers since. She lives in Derbyshire with her husband and their two children. Her latest novel, *Gallery Girl*, is out now.

CATHY KELLY is a number one bestselling author. She worked as a journalist before becoming a novelist, and has published twelve bestselling books. She is also an ambassador for UNICEF in Ireland. She lives in Wicklow with her husband,

John, and their twin sons, Murray and Dylan. Please visit www.cathykelly.com for more information on Cathy Kelly.

DOUGLAS KENNEDY's novels include the critically acclaimed bestsellers *The Big Picture* and *The Pursuit of Happiness*. He is also the author of three travel books and his work has been translated into twenty-two languages. In 2006, he was awarded the French decoration of Chevalier de l'Ordre des Arts et des Lettres. Born in Manhattan in 1955, he has two children and currently divides his time between London, Paris and Maine. His latest novel, published in 2011, is *The Moment*.

SOPHIE KINSELLA lives in London with her husband and four sons. Having graduated from Oxford, she worked as a financial journalist, before writing the smash hit *The Secret Dreamworld of a Shopaholic*, which has been adapted into a film. The latest addition to the *Shopaholic* series, *Mini Shopaholic* is out now.

SANTA MONTEFIORE's books have been translated into twenty languages, and over two million copies have been sold throughout Europe and America. *The House by The Sea*, out this July, is her eleventh novel. Santa was born in England in 1970 and read Spanish and Italian at Exeter University. She lives in London with her husband, the writer and historian Simon Sebag Montefiore, and their children Lily and Sasha.

JANE MOORE is a columnist for the *Sun* and *GQ* magazine and presents documentaries including Channel 4's *Dispatches*. She has also made regular appearances on shows including *Loose Women* and *Grumpy Old Women*. Jane is the bestselling author of *The Second Wives Club* and *Perfect Match*. She lives in London with her husband and daughters. *Love is On the Air* is out now.

KATE MOSSE is the author of two non-fiction books, one play and five novels, including the number one international bestsellers, *Labyrinth*, *Sepulchre* and *The Winter Ghosts*. The co-founder of the Orange Prize for Fiction, she is one of the authors campaigning against library closures in the UK and is on the steering committee for WOW, the international women's arts festival based at the South Bank Centre in London. A member of the Board of the National Theatre and a Trustee of the Weald & Downland Open Air Museum in Sussex, Kate is currently working on a book celebrating the 50th Anniversary of Chichester Festival Theatre, a major play commission and the final novel in her Languedoc Trilogy, *Citadel*, which will be published in 2012.

JOJO MOYES began her writing career as a journalist at the *Independent*, where she worked for ten years. She published her first novel, *Sheltering Rain*, in 2002 and has been a full-time novelist ever since. Jojo lives on a farm in Essex with her husband and their three children. Her latest novel, *The Last Letter from Your Lover*, is out now.

FIONA NEILL is a novelist and journalist. After working abroad for six years as a foreign correspondent in Latin America, she returned to the UK to become assistant editor at *Marie Claire* and then *The Times Magazine*. She now lives in London with her husband and three children. Her first novel, *The Secret Life of a Slummy Mummy*, was an instant bestseller. This was followed by *Friends, Lovers and Other Indiscretions*, which also became a *Sunday Times* bestseller. Her third novel, *What the Nanny Saw*, about a penniless student who goes to work for a wealthy but dysfunctional banking family, is out now.

ELIZABETH NOBLE's first novel, *The Reading Group*, was published in 2004, and became an international bestseller and a *Sunday Times* number one. All of her subsequent novels, *The Friendship Test*, *Alphabet Weekends*, *Things I Want My Daughters to Know*, and *The Girl Next Door*, were also *Sunday Times* top ten titles, and her latest novel, *The Way We Were*, is published in paperback this summer. Married, with two daughters, Elizabeth divides her time between homes in New York City and Guildford, Surrey.

ADELE PARKS was born in Teesside. She published her first novel, *Playing Away*, in 2000 and was the debut best seller of that year. She has since published nine more *Sunday Times* top ten bestsellers, including *Husbands* and *Men I've Loved Before*. Her latest novel, *About Last Night* is published in 2011. Adele is translated into over twenty different languages. She writes regularly for magazines and newspapers and in 2010 was a judge for the Costa Book Awards. To learn more about Adele visit www.adeleparks.com or follow her on Twitter @adeleparks

JODI PICOULT is the bestselling author of eighteen novels, of which the most recent four debuted at number one on the *New York Times* bestseller list. After studying creative writing at Princeton, Picoult had various jobs, including technical writer for a Wall Street brokerage firm and 8th grade English teacher, before pursuing a master's in education at Harvard. She has won numerous awards including a lifetime achievement award for mainstream fiction from the Romance Writers of America and Waterstone's Author of the Year in the UK. Her books are published in thirty-five countries and *My Sister's Keeper* was made into a film starring Cameron Diaz. Jodi lives with her husband and three children in New Hampshire. Her latest novel, *Sing You Home*, is published in 2011.

RUTH RENDELL has written over seventy crime novels since her first publication in 1964. She is the creator of the bestselling Chief Inspector Wexford series and has won numerous awards for her writing. Ruth was awarded a CBE in 1996 and currently sits in the House of Lords as a working peer. She lives in London. Her most recent novels are *Tigerlily's Orchids* and a new Wexford novel, *The Vault*.

LOUISE SHARLAND was originally from Montreal, Canada and moved to the UK after falling in love with a British sailor. Always a voracious reader, she started writing seriously fifteen years ago, when at home with two young children, and in 2001 was short-listed for the *Mail on Sunday*'s Novel Writing Competition. In 2006 Louise began teaching creative writing evening classes, and in 2010 won the *woman&home* short story competition. She is now working on a full length novel entitled *The Final Rite*, a psychological thriller based loosely on the play *Electra*, exploring the age old themes of revenge and redemption.

CATRIONA STEWART has lived and worked in mid Wales for a quarter of a century. After a professional career in housing and social services, where she occasionally made time for writing during career breaks with four children, she took early retirement and can now write as much as she wants, which means pretty much all the time. She's also a regular face in her local libraries. She's been successful in various fiction writing competitions, including a first prize in the *woman&home* annual short story competition in 2009. She's working on a novel, or two, as well.

ALISON WEIR was born in London and now resides in Surrey. Before becoming a published author in 1989, she was a civil servant, then a housewife and mother. From 1991 to 1997, whilst researching and writing books, she ran a school for children with learning difficulties before taking up writing full time. Her non-fiction books include *The Six Wives of Henry VIII*, *Lancaster and York*, *Children of England*, *Elizabeth the Queen*, *Eleanor of Aquitaine*, *Mary, Queen of Scots and the Murder of Lord Darnley*, *Henry VIII: King and Court*, *Isabella*, *Katherine Swynford*, *The Lady in the Tower* and her latest biography *Mary Boleyn*. She is also the author of bestselling novels including *Innocent Traitor*, *The Lady Elizabeth* and *The Captive Queen*.

Foreword

BY BREAST CANCER CARE
AMBASSADOR, MEERA SYAL MBE

*I*t's a real honour to be asked to introduce this book full of wonderful stories from such talented authors. I love reading and I am truly passionate about the work of Breast Cancer Care so for me, this collection of short stories is a match made in heaven! I can indulge my love of reading whilst helping a very special charity and I hope many of you will do the same too.

woman&home magazine has been a staunch supporter of Breast Cancer Care for nine years and has now helped raise £5.5 million to ensure the charity can continue its invaluable work supporting people affected by breast cancer. And for every copy of this book sold, Breast Cancer Care will receive £1 towards their vital services which are all provided for free.

My Mum has had breast cancer so I know how vital Breast Cancer Care's support and information can be for anyone faced with this dreadful disease. They offer a helping hand not only to the person diagnosed but also offer support to their friends and families who are terrified and distraught on hearing a loved one has breast cancer. Thanks to the support of *woman&home*,

and all its readers, so many more people have benefited from Breast Cancer Care free services all over the country.

If you, or anyone you know needs help with breast cancer, please do point them in the right direction. A good place to start is the website www.breastcancer care.org.uk or the free Helpline 0808 800 6000.

In the meantime, curl up with this delightful book safe in the knowledge that you are helping thousands of people at the same time. Enjoy!

the
Best
Little Book Club
in Town

Stories by
ELIZABETH BUCHAN, LEE CHILD,
KATIE FFORDE, SOPHIE KINSELLA,
KATE MOSSE, ELIZABETH NOBLE,
JODI PICOULT
and many more . . .

EDITED BY FANNY BLAKE
FOR
woman&home

An Orion Paperback
First published in Great Britain in 2011
by Orion Books
an imprint of the Orion Publishing Group Ltd
Orion House, 5 Upper St Martin's Lane,
London, WC2H 9EA

An Hachette UK company

10 9 8 7 6 5 4 3

Compilation copyright © The Orion Publishing Group Ltd, 2011
For copyright of individual stories please see pgs 315–16

All stories have previously been published in *woman&home* magazine.

A CIP catalogue record for this book
is available from the British Library.

ISBN 978 1 4091 3660 6

Typeset at The Spartan Press Ltd,
Lymington, Hants

Printed in Great Britain by Clays Ltd, St Ives plc

The Orion Publishing Group's policy is to use papers
that are natural, renewable and recyclable products and
made from wood grown in sustainable forests. The logging
and manufacturing processes are expected to conform to
the environmental regulations of the country of origin.

www.orionbooks.co.uk

Contents

Rising by Naomi Alderman   1

Needs Must by Elizabeth Buchan   9

Twelve Per Cent by Tess Callahan   19

A Remnant from the Past by Mavis Cheek   31

The Ammonite by Tracy Chevalier   41

Grit in My Eye by Lee Child   49

A Night Out by Helen Dunmore   59

The Promotion by Jane Fallon   69

Breakfast with Mr Gillyflower by Katie Fforde   77

The Bench by Esther Freud   89

The Whole Truth and Nothing But the Truth
   by Tess Gerritsen   97

The Coiled Serpent by Daisy Goodwin   107

The Safety Net by Sophie Hannah   117

Sweet Peas by Rachel Heath   125

The Naked Truth by Wendy Holden   135

Four Days to Christmas by Cathy Kelly   145

Sonata d'Été by Douglas Kennedy   151

Christmas List by Sophie Kinsella   161

A Small Adventure by Santa Montefiore   175

Radio Waves by Jane Moore   185

The House on the Hill by Kate Mosse   195
Crocodile Shoes by Jojo Moyes   205
Quality Time by Fiona Neill   215
Sunny Aspect by Elizabeth Noble   227
Grating Expectations by Adele Parks   235
Ritz by Jodi Picoult   245
The Wrong Category by Ruth Rendell   271
Black Rock by Louise Sharland   281
The Rain in Spain by Catriona Stewart   293
The Anniversary by Alison Weir   303

Rising

BY NAOMI ALDERMAN

'*I* am embarking on a new venture.'

'I am already successful and becoming more so.'

'I am a valuable woman in my own right.'

Laura stared at the Post-it notes on her bathroom mirror and thought, Yes, but I'm also single again, fat and terrified.

She breathed in, breathed out, pulled the Post-it notes off the mirror and threw them into the bin. She looked at herself.

'I don't care,' she said out loud to her reflection, 'what kind of a woman I am or how successful. I'm doing this because I have to and because I can't think of anything else to do.'

She pulled on her coat and left.

It wasn't meant to be this way. The bakery was her dream with Pete. They'd planned it together, found the perfect spot, a small commuter town with easy links to London, a pretty high street, the owner of a little restaurant retiring. This was supposed to be the start of their new life, with Pete quitting his job, the two of them starting to work together and having more time as a couple in the evening.

Except it hadn't gone that way. When it came to quitting his job, Pete had become more and more vague. This month wasn't the right time. If he just waited a bit longer there'd be a bonus. Maybe he could continue to work in town and she could start up the bakery, and he'd commute?

She had been sympathetic. Hard for a man to give up his career. Hard for someone in his forties to change tack. She'd been so stupid. It hadn't been his dedication to his career, and it hadn't been the bonus. It had been Rachel the junior executive, in the bathroom, after the Christmas party. And then again, in the New Year. And then again. And then again. And then again. Who was it who said that having sex is a relationship if you just do it enough times? Pete, possibly.

And when Laura had cried so much that she had bored herself with tears, and talked to her friends so much that she'd worn out all her words, and obsessed over everything he'd said so much that she'd become tired of thinking about him, it was then that she looked at the loan agreements and the rental contracts. And she'd seen that it was her name, not his, on everything. He'd always been too busy (doing what?) or too tired (from what?) to come to those important signing meetings. So now it was her bakery. Her new chance. Her fresh start.

I'm doing this, she said to herself, because I can't

think of anything else to do. But that's all right. Probably.

There was, she found, something soothing about the work, in any case. Up at five, just as the pre-dawn light was beginning to trickle across the ink-blue sky. Trying not to think of Pete and their early morning routine, leaving the house quickly, unlocking the bakery while the streets were still dark, turning on the back-room lights, starting the coffee machine and kneading the dough.

It was the dough in particular that she found herself longing for as if it were a lover. Perhaps it was the rhythm, knead-stretch, knead-stretch, that emptied her mind of all thoughts, that meant that when a thought of Pete arose she could pummel it into the dough until it dissipated. Perhaps it was the simplicity of it.

She had a mixing machine, with dough hooks and special bread cycles. But she found that she preferred to knead herself, elbows deep in the warm fleshiness, floury and smelling of yeast. Plunging her arms into the dough, she thought of the generations, the centuries of people who had made bread like this. Leaving it to rise and then prove, she felt a certain nurturing, a sense that everything had its time and order, that nothing needed to be rushed. Shaping soft handfuls into rolls, placing them in the oven, removing them hot and crusty and smelling of nourishment, she experienced a satisfying feeling of strength. Bread is powerful, she thought, as the first customers of the day arrived.

The days were busy. She'd been right: this was a high street without a local bakery, without somewhere for people to sit and have a coffee, some toast or a slice of cake. A few curious visitors on the first day turned into a trickle, then became a steady stream of regulars.

There were Maureen and Roger, a couple in their sixties, stopping off after walking their dogs, and Susie and Michelle, friends, each with a toddler in tow, meeting for a gossip after the school run. There was Daniel, an architect working from home who wanted to escape the same four walls, and Rosalie, a retired headmistress who sat in the corner and read, seemingly, a book a day. And it was good. None of her regulars had known Pete and she didn't tell any of them her life story. Just 'I wanted to start again': that was all. Everyone wanted that.

During the days, she worked. From the early morning, she was kneading and rolling, baking blind, filling tart cases and buttering baps. When the customers began to arrive, she was occupied with their needs, chatting to them, hearing their stories. At the end of the day there was cleaning up, sorting, entering the day's takings in the book, considering which recipes had been successful and which not.

In the evenings, though, after the bustle of the day was done, she found herself drifting into her bedroom, glass of wine in hand, and staring at her body. There it was. Muffin top and soft thighs. Portly stomach, dimpled flesh. Pete had always liked it but . . . Pete was gone, and who would love this soft fleshy body now? She jabbed a finger into her stomach, watching the flesh crease around it. She grabbed her muffin top with one hand and squeezed. She considered diets, exercise, but knew that she was just too busy for all that weighing and measuring, and too tired to pound the treadmill after work. Her body sometimes seemed to her simply rolls upon rolls, but there it was, and perhaps no lover would ever touch it again.

She began to go to bed earlier so as not to face these late-night thoughts. She woke earlier too, and more easily. Out of bed at four-thirty without difficulty, sharing the early-morning summer sunlight with an insomniac dog walker or two, earlier, even, than the milkman and the paper-girl. Arriving early at the bakery, she had time to experiment. She rolled the corners of soft pastry triangles to make croissants: almond and chocolate, then also cinnamon, apricot, peach. She dug her hands into the yielding dough and formed the damp spheres of rolls: white, granary and wholewheat, cheese, and also caraway, red onion, mustard-seed.

Her regulars increased in number, slowly but steadily. There was Margot now, a woman in her fifties often tapping away at her laptop, and Alexander, a local estate agent but nice enough even so, always ducking out of the shop to make a phone call on the pavement. It surprised her to learn that they wanted her to succeed.

'This town's needed somewhere like this for ever,'

said Rosalie, collecting her slice of lemon drizzle and retiring to her corner nook.

Maureen and Roger nodded in unison.

'We don't know what we did before we started coming here, do we, Roger?'

'No, weren't we just saying that the other day, Maureen? You've been a godsend.'

'It's true,' said Daniel. He was usually so quiet, working on his papers or staring out at the people walking past. He looked at her now, though, and she noticed that his eyes were very blue. Bright, clear blue. 'It's true,' he said again, 'we're glad you've come.'

Margot, it transpired, was a local journalist. She hadn't mentioned it, didn't even say anything on the day that the piece she'd written about Laura's bakery was published. She just sat at her usual table, eating her usual hot buttered roll and fruit salad, saying nothing at all until Maureen and Roger arrived, brandishing the paper, open to the review page.

'Look!' said Maureen. 'New bakery wows locals with inventive recipes.'

'Yes,' said Roger. 'The caraway seed buns are a particular delight.'

Margot blinked and smiled.

'Why didn't you say anything?' said Maureen. 'You could have got Laura excited about it! And, anyway, you've only had the caraway buns once!'

'Once was all it took,' said Margot.

'You can tell just by looking that they're delicious,' said Daniel, softly.

6

Laura cut out the article, had it laminated and put it in the window. There were others soon enough. Five stars from the county paper. Recommendations from local food and tourist guides. It wasn't just regulars now; there were orders from across the county. She still rose in the early mornings to knead the dough and bake the pastry cases.

I'll have to take on an assistant soon, she thought, and realised she would miss the solitude of the dawn, her arms deep in warm, living bread dough. The texture of it was delicious beneath her fingertips, the yielding, soft, wholesome mound comforting to the touch.

In the evenings, she looked at her body. She was fat. There was no denying it. She closed her eyes and ran her fingers down her torso, feeling the ripples of flesh. She noticed that her skin was very soft, her body warm and supple. Eyes still closed, she rubbed her belly. It was round and generous. Like the dough, her body was plump, overflowing, delicious. Like the dough, it was comforting and perhaps, yes, enticing. She opened her eyes. Something had changed.

The next morning, Daniel was the first to arrive at the bakery, just as she flipped the sign from 'closed' to 'open'. He seemed nervous, jiggling slightly from foot to foot as he ordered, yes, his usual, no, how about the caramel cake, no, maybe one of the scones, no, well, perhaps some toast. She laughed.

'Don't know what you want, eh?'

And he looked at her with his very blue eyes, and the

soft curls falling across his forehead, and said, 'Maybe I do know.'

'Yes?' she said, and suddenly her heart was full of anticipation.

He gulped.

'I've always wanted,' he said, 'to learn to make pastry.'

'Well then,' said Laura, 'you should come back to the shop this evening and I'll teach you.'

He arrived, again, as soon as she flipped the sign back from 'open' to 'closed'. He'd brought a bottle of wine 'for a nervous student', and she smiled. She laid out the ingredients. He told her, in gabbles, about his work, his hopes, his plans for the future. He was younger than her but ambitious and interested in the world. Yes, she thought, I like you.

She showed him how to rub the fat into the flour. Lift, rub, drop. Aerate the mixture. Blend in the water, drop by drop. No, not like that.

She stood behind to demonstrate, felt the strength in his arms as he worked. He turned around. His hands were covered with flour, even his face was slightly dusted. He looked at her, his expression serious. And he leaned in towards her and she leaned towards him. And as they kissed, his floury hands moved across her ample hips, her round stomach, her breasts. And she found herself thinking that the top of a muffin is a generous and delicious thing. And all dough really needs to rise is time.

Needs Must

BY ELIZABETH BUCHAN

*P*lum Talbot regarded the tall, slightly too thin, but graceful thirty-something man across the jib and jabber of Ettie's party.

That's him. He's perfect.

It didn't take more than that. A woman who had primed her instincts to remain on full alert, Plum was entirely familiar with the prickles at the back of her neck as they activated.

Ettie, at full tilt, whisked past her with a plate of canapés. Plum clutched at her arm. 'Hey,' said Ettie, as the canapés see-sawed. 'Careful.'

'Who he?' Plum asked. 'Important. Very.'

'Who?' Ettie's gaze raked over the guests. 'Oh, him. David Duke. Moved in opposite. Top life coach and therapist. Single.' She sobered. 'Wife killed in a cycle accident. Terrible.'

Plum snatched up a canapé and ate it. The contrast between the fleshy cherry tomato and the pâté was well judged – one of Lottie's specialities. 'I love you, Ettie.'

Ettie flung her a frazzled look. 'Wish this was over.'

'No, you don't.'

All the same, and in the spirit of friendship, Plum went around the room checking the candles and chivvying stragglers towards the buffet table.

As she did so, she observed David Duke who was waiting quietly to help himself. Yet his was not a passive stance. No, David Duke was watching the guests, an activity that seemed to be of immense interest and significance to him.

A woman in a tight black dress came up to him and laid a hand on his arm. 'You're the best, David.'

Plum couldn't quite see his expression, but she heard the reply. 'Charlie got there of his own accord.'

The woman smiled. 'Even so.' Her attitude implied gratitude and trust.

An echo sounded in Plum's head – of unresolved grief and longing. For wholeness, she thought. That's what.

Before she could move into action, David Duke's mobile rang. He answered it, murmured, 'Don't worry, I'll come,' and headed for Ettie. She watched him apologise, kiss Ettie's cheek and move towards the door.

Then he was gone.

Before she left, Plum cornered Ettie. The party was over, the pretty dining room was littered with dirty glasses and plates, and the candles had burned dangerously low.

'Where can I contact him?'

'What are you up to, Plum? Thought you distrusted that sort of stuff.'

I do. I do. Plum raised her eyebrows, gave a tiny shrug. 'It's not for me,' she said.

'Oh, never mind. I can see you're not going to tell me. I'll text you the number.' Ettie's tiredness sharpened into pique. 'The things I do for you.'

Plum kissed her.

David Duke's waiting room was as neutrally soothing and contained the same fatigued selection of magazines as most waiting rooms.

Handbag on knee as defensive rampart, Plum waited. Her nerves were shot and the instinct on which she has prided herself had taken a rain check. Sure, she could tell herself that no one wins if they don't dare as many times as there were daisies on her lawn, but it wouldn't hide her vulnerability.

'Hello.' David Duke got to his feet when Plum entered the room. He frowned. 'Have we already met?'

'No.'

As with so much in her life, it wasn't quite a lie, but it also wasn't quite the truth. Anxious to pick up some clues about him, she glanced around, but was met with the same studied blandness of the waiting room. No photograph. No pot plant. Nothing.

He indicated a chair. His smile was warm and thoughtful, and she found herself smiling back.

'I'd like to ask why you are here and what you hope to gain from the session.'

Plum could think of several answers – none of which were necessary to share with David Duke.

'Life has been a bit complicated and I need to sort out a new direction.'

He pulled a notepad towards him. 'Go on.'

Plum swallowed. 'My husband and I got divorced four years ago, and my business has recently folded.'

'Any particular complications?'

Plum bristled. 'Isn't that enough?'

His hand stilled on the notepad. 'Isn't that why you're here? Do you have children?'

'Two. Lottie and Ben.'

'And?'

The recollection was immediate. Lottie's choking sobs, which she struggled to stifle, tore through her mother. 'Lottie, what is it?' Not that Plum didn't already know.

'Joe . . .'

'Ah, Joe.'

The latest in a series of beautiful boys whom dewy, honeypot Lottie fell in love with, Joe had done a runner.

'A month ago he wanted to marry me. Now, he says he decided that he has to find himself in Thailand.'

If she could have murdered Joe, Plum would have done so. With extreme savagery. Instead, weeping inwardly for her daughter, she dried Lottie's tears, heated up a bowl of consommé, forced Lottie to down it and issued the advice she should have given two boyfriends ago.

'You need an older man, Lottie. Not a golden youth. Golden youths don't want what you want. Until their looks fade, they are spoiled and short-sighted.' She caressed Lottie's wet cheek. 'It's natural. If you look like a god, you act like one.'

Lottie said, 'I don't think I'm cut out for happiness.'

Plum's heart contorted painfully. 'Just because Joe is a fool, there's no reason to jump to that conclusion.'

Lottie said, 'All I want to do is to have babies, make jam and sew quilts but, apparently, this is deranged thinking, particularly since I'm running a successful business. When did this happen?'

'My generation,' said Plum.

'Well,' said Lottie crossly, 'looks as though you exchanged one millstone around the neck for another.'

'Plum . . . May I call you Plum?' David Duke was observing her with the diligent intelligence she had noted at Ettie's party. 'Could we begin?'

Plum was panicking at her own stupidity. She had nothing to say. Everything was done and dusted. Boxed up. Supposing that she might confide a little, just a little, in someone . . . Wild horses normally would not induce her to do so to a stranger, even if he did have kind eyes.

Then, she thought of Lottie and of what needed to be done.

'As I said, there was a divorce, then our financial consulting website went—'

'Wrong?'

Plum pulled at her forefinger. Bad habit.

'Jem and I were reasonably well known in the City. Then I discovered that he had fiddled the accounts. He hadn't defrauded the clients, luckily. Only me. That was a shock.'

As if it were yesterday, she reprised the assault that the news had unleashed on her body when everything – heart, pulse, blood – thudded and shuddered.

'It was a cushion for when he left, he informed me.' Pause. 'Which he told me he had been planning to do for some time.'

'And?'

Why hadn't she thought this through? She steadied herself. Lottie, Lottie, my daughter in trouble.

'I couldn't believe that the kind, honest man whom I thought I was married to – wasn't.'

'How did you cope?'

Plum shrugged. 'The business fell apart. Word got around and clients deserted in droves. They always do at the slightest suggestion of something wrong.'

'And did you fall apart?'

'No. No.' She brushed a strand of hair away from her face.

David Duke took a note. 'Do you keep in touch with Jem?'

Long silence. 'Yes.'

'I deduce that contact is difficult. Naturally.' More note taking. 'Should we talk over how this could be improved?'

A rising panic stopped her tongue for a few seconds. 'That might be a good idea.'

'You don't sound sure.' A pause. 'And the children?'

'Ben is tutoring in Saudi.'

Carrying that ridiculous suitcase into the airport. Then . . . vanishing.

'He felt he had to get out of the country. Whereas Lottie—'

'How did you feel about Ben leaving?' David Duke cut in.

'Fine.' Plum searched in her handbag. 'Sad-ish. No . . .'

She produced a card and was brought up short by David Duke's evident scepticism.

'OK.' She felt her lips go dry. 'I was anguished, but this is Lottie. She's running a cookery business. She looks after me, now Ben's gone. Casserole, the name of her catering business, is going well. But she's—'

Again he interrupted. 'We're here to talk about you.' David Duke smiled to neutralise any sting. 'Tell me about the divorce. Are things reasonably settled and equable? How do you feel about it?'

'Fine. I'm more worried about the children. Lottie is very good—'

He looked at Plum.

'I must ask you to concentrate if we are to make something of this session.' He switched tactics. 'Have you lost weight recently?'

Plum was startled. 'Actually, I have.'

'Are you sleeping OK?'

'Not terrifically well.'

His questions, which she knew she should have anticipated but hadn't, punctured the careful front that she had put up for so long. Stop, please, she wanted to tell him. I don't mean to be here. It's not for me.

'Are you working again? I imagine it's taken a bit of time to disentangle things.' If possible, his eyes seemed even kindlier. 'It's difficult to retrieve a business reputation once it's lost.'

'That's true. And it's been a nightmare putting it right.'

'And your ex-husband is doing well?'

There was now a very long silence as Plum struggled for mastery. Pain. Despair. Outrage.

'That's it, he is. He's up and running professionally, and with someone else.'

Did I go mad? Yes, yes I did, a little.

'That was hard too. I couldn't accept that he had recovered so quickly . . . You see, I didn't.'

'Have you talked to anyone about your position?'

The session was sliding out of Plum's grasp and with it her self-control, her grip on her brittle and precarious make-believe.

'Lottie. She's wonderful. I can talk to her about most things.'

'But not everything?'

'No.'

'For example, that you are angry with her father?'

She frowned at him. 'Exactly.'

'Because you might be derogatory about him.'

A reluctant smile tugged at Plum's mouth. 'I thought I was supposed to be giving the answers.'

His chair swivelled as he got up. 'I think you are at

the hardest stage of a long process of readjustment. I would like to suggest a visualisation exercise that might help.'

Long process?

'Don't worry, this is not batty, all things being equal. Where would you like to be?'

'Somewhere warm.'

'Wearing what?'

'A big red skirt and a T-shirt.'

'Shut your eyes, put them on and start walking towards a point in the distance. It is beautifully warm. You are perfectly relaxed and you are breathing deeply and evenly. Concentrate on that feeling of well-being.'

Plum breathed in. She felt dangerously fragile. The worries, the future . . . How could she bring Lottie back into the conversation? Oh the jostle and aches of her unquiet mind, the hurts and the wounds . . .

Her eyelids flicked open and she found herself staring straight at David Duke.

'Plum,' said David, 'you didn't really want to consult me. So why did you?'

To Plum's shock, she began to cry. 'I'm so sorry . . .'

He pushed a box of tissues in her direction. 'It's not unknown,' he said gently and waited for her to stop.

But Plum didn't stop. She couldn't, and she cried and cried, and all the grief of the past few years flowed with the tears, leaving her broken and winded in David Duke's consulting room.

Eventually, he said, 'Someone should come and collect you.' He glanced at Lottie's business card on his desk. 'Your daughter perhaps? And, with your permission, I would like a quick word with her.'

Between the gasping, cathartic, oh-so-necessary sobs, Plum felt the inestimable pleasure of a nail banged on the head.

'You didn't?' said Ettie.

Plum looked smug.

'And it's worked?'

'Seems to have done. She's cooking him dinner this evening.'

'But how did you do it? You can't just walk into a consulting room and demand your daughter is taken on a date.'

Plum considered. In all sorts of ways, she felt so much better.

'My instincts,' she replied. 'I acted on them,' she added. 'My instincts as a mother.'

Twelve Per Cent

BY TESS CALLAHAN

O utside the hospital, the dog looked up at Cecilia with a question in his eyes.

'Hold on. Let's get our bearings,' Cecilia said. 'You know how these visits can be.'

She sat on a bench and strapped on the special vest that labelled him as a therapy dog. Fury gave a single, dignified wave of his tail and turned towards the entrance. The automatic doors glided open and a nurse appeared, lighting a cigarette.

'Hey, pet therapy day,' she said, kneeling down to tousle the dog's coat. 'Collie-retriever mix?'

'Anyone's guess,' Cecilia said. 'Dog-shelter speciality.'

'God, he's soft. You know, the staff need these dogs more than the patients do,' she said, exhaling smoke.

'Me most of all,' Cecilia said.

As she signed in at the front desk, she reminded herself to keep an eye on her watch. She could stay for forty-five minutes, tops. Although she had instructed her children to finish packing in her absence, she pictured them at this moment texting their friends over a bowl of cereal or creating new playlists on their iPods.

'If only you could train them as well as the dog,' her husband often said.

Before leaving the house, Cecilia had argued with them about the condition of their rooms. This, after an entire school year of nagging about homework, piano, sports, choir and play rehearsal. Cecilia knew she was living a harried life; it bothered her that she was teaching her kids to do the same.

After the pet therapy visit, she would stop by her mother's flat to make sure the refrigerator was stocked and prescriptions refilled. Cecilia could no longer take a week's holiday without worrying about the consequences.

On top of this, she had to turn in her school reports for year six by midnight tonight. She had already averaged out the marks; it was the comments that weighed on her. What could she possibly write about Tommy Francis? Your darling son swallowed our class goldfish? Little Tommy needs a straitjacket? No, she would have to be more tactful. She would take her laptop in the car, try to finish the reports by the time they reached the cottage and email them before the deadline, assuming she could find Internet service.

Yesterday, while eating a sandwich in the staff room, punching numbers into her calculator and glancing at her emails, she tasted a piece of pickle on her tongue, squeaky and bright. She had forgotten about the pickle. In fact, she had no idea what she was eating.

How much of her day was spent that way, shoving through things unconsciously? It was a kind of insanity. She might be known as the volunteer who visits the local loony bin once a month with her dog, but, in truth, she was the crazy one.

The bell rang. She was late for class.

Fury gave a little shake and looked over his shoulder at her. What were they waiting for? They started down the hall. As a new volunteer, Cecilia used to go to the Voluntary Ward for patients who willingly admitted themselves. Now she had graduated to the Involuntary Unit, a dubious promotion. At the entrance to the ward, she pushed the intercom button.

'Paws for People,' Cecilia said. 'I'm here with Fury.'

There was no response, but in a moment the door opened and a heavy-set, exhausted-looking nurse let her in.

'We told the dog phobics to stay in their rooms,' she said. 'The others are in the visitors' lounge waiting for you. We've rounded up some real crackpots for you today.'

The nurse's dark humour unnerved Cecilia, though she understood the need for it.

In the lounge, patients sat in a random circle. They had the appearance of being placed in their chairs just so, like giant sacks of sand adjusted this way or that to keep from tumbling over. An older man with a groomed goatee snored in his seat. An overweight woman sitting across two folding chairs smoothed her tent dress down over her knees again and again in an effort to iron out wrinkles. A middle-aged woman with a sharp jaw and an outbreak of acne was talking incessantly.

'He yours? What's his name? Does he do tricks? I raise circus dogs. What's his name?'

Over the years, Cecilia had learned to let Fury decide whom to approach. Almost without fail, the nurses told her, the dog went to the most disturbed person first. Fury ignored the compulsive talker and nosed his way to a young girl with long plaits sitting on the floor. She looked no older than Cecilia's daughter, but since she was not in the paediatric ward, she had to be at least nineteen.

'Hi, there. I'm Cecilia,' she said. 'And this is Fury.'

Fury craned his nose to within inches of the girl's mouth. She laughed, giving him the whiff of breath he was hoping for. He often found the singed, medicated scent of the patients' breath worth studying.

'So soft,' the girl said, raking her fingers through his coat.

She had an easy, unencumbered smile. Fury moved his snout down the girl's sleeve to her wrist. He became still, only his whiskers moving. The girl offered the other wrist as well, held out as if she wore hand-cuffs to be unlocked. She watched as he investigated each one carefully, without rushing. When he was done, he put his nose into her hair and gave a little snort. She giggled and began petting him again. Only when Cecilia looked did she notice the flash of white gauze beneath the girl's cuffs.

'I have a dog,' the girl said. 'But he has short hair. You can't get your fingers through it like this.'

'Fury loves attention,' Cecilia said. 'Right now, you're his best friend.'

'Mine's a Rottweiler,' she said. 'Everyone's scared of him, but he's just a big softie.'

'Does he do tricks?' the incessant talker said. 'I used to raise show dogs. I taught them to walk on the ceiling.'

'His name is Tinker Bell,' the girl said. 'It's a joke name, you know, because he's over a hundred pounds.'

'I like it,' Cecilia said. 'Fury's name is ironic, too. The only thing he's furious about is chasing squirrels.'

'Bet he's fast,' the girl said. 'I miss Tinky. I miss him so badly.'

'He sounds like a great dog.'

'Yeah, well, he has this thing with fire engines. When he hears the siren he goes ballistic. Tries to get out the window. He's gouged out all the windowsills. It's bad because we live down the street from the fire station. My mum's boyfriend was going to have him put down. Like, really. The dog needs a tranquilliser or something, or maybe earplugs. Do they sell doggie earplugs?'

'If they don't, they should.'

The chronic talker kept on. 'I taught them to walk straight up the walls to the ceiling and do backflips up there.'

The girl with the plaits leaned her forehead against Fury's. 'You'd better say hi to the others or they'll get

23

pissed off,' she said. 'People aren't as forgiving as dogs.'

The woman in the tent dress rocked back and forth, causing the folding chairs to creak. With the flat of her hand, she repeatedly pressed down the fabric on her thigh. Fury put his chin tentatively on her knee. She regarded him slowly, as if noticing only then that she was not alone in the room.

'I'm Cecilia, and this is Fury; we're here for a visit.'

The woman did not look up, but lifted her hand to the dog's head. Cecilia worried that she would apply the same heavy pressure as she had to her dress, but she touched Fury lightly, feeling the velvety tips of his ears. Her eyes, focused on the dog, became less empty. When Fury's nose left a small wet spot on the dress, she pushed him away and rubbed the spot with anxious fingers.

'Sorry about that,' Cecilia said. 'It should dry in no time.'

The dog moved to the sleeping man and touched his fingers, dangling from an armrest. The man did not startle, but gradually opened his eyes and took in the animal.

'Hi, there. I'm Cecilia and this is my dog.'

The man lifted his head and looked Cecilia in the eye. He had a gentle, intelligent gaze full of immense sadness. He said nothing but nodded appreciatively. Fury sat beside him. The man caressed him, finding the sweet spot behind his ear. The dog leaned into him, giving himself over. For a moment the man and the dog belonged to each other.

'Bring it here,' the talker said.

The man withdrew his hand and allowed them to move on. Except for the talker, the patients sat in silence. There were no magazines, no mobile phones, no attempts at conversation. Each person sat alone with his thoughts, or the absence of them.

'Yes, yes,' the talker said as they approached. 'Cecily and Furious. I got it. What a handsome dog. Nice aura, too. You can see right through it, like clean water. But yours,' she said, addressing Cecilia. 'Yours is mucky, like your mind's got an algae bloom growing inside it.'

The woman did not touch the dog, who was glancing back at the girl with the plaits.

'It's a time problem, isn't it?' the talker said. 'See, the dog is outside time. I mean, sure, he's born, he lives, and he dies, but moment to moment he's never not here. So, since the present moment is the only one we ever have, he's actually immortal. Whereas you,' she said to Cecilia, 'you're only about twelve per cent here. Which means eighty-eight per cent of you is down the toilet.'

'Hey, this is a visitor,' said the large woman in the tent dress. 'She's a volunteer. Can you give her a little respect?'

'Don't worry,' the nurse told Cecilia. 'She told me I'm ninety-five per cent dead. It's amazing I'm able to walk around on five per cent humanity.'

'I'm leaving on holiday this afternoon,' Cecilia said

to the talker. 'We're not packed yet. Maybe that's why I seem preoccupied.'

'Holiday? Where to?' said the talker.

Immediately, Cecilia realised her mistake. 'Just up to the Lakes for some hiking.' How must it feel for these locked-up people to hear about her holiday?

'Is Rage going with you?'

'Fury,' Cecilia said. 'Yes, he's the only one who's ready.'

'Go ahead, go on holiday; it won't make any difference. You see, the dog is free even though he's on a lead, whereas you're confined because your thoughts are thick. They went from fine and wispy when you were a girl, to soupier as a young woman, and now, well, take a look. They're like calcified rock. Your head's in a cave made of your own assumptions.'

Cecilia bristled. Assumptions like what? That she was obliged to care for her mother, her children and her students? To make appointments for oil changes and dentist appointments? To cook dinner and do laundry? Were any of these things negotiable?

'A dog could have a hundred things to do in a day – a police dog, let's say – and still be equally present to all of them,' the woman said. 'Your problem isn't that you haven't packed; it's that you've overpacked. Your brain, that is.'

Cecilia let the lead go slack and the dog quietly made its way back to the girl with the plaits. Fury rolled onto his back for a belly rub and the girl beamed down at him.

Cecilia ought to go. She still had to stop the post, water the plants and, dear God, do the reports. Dear Mrs Francis, Tommy interrupts more than any child I have ever taught. Every moment in the classroom with him makes me want to jump out the window like a raving lunatic. No, that wouldn't do.

'Nice to have met you,' Cecilia said to the talker.

The woman kept on speaking while Cecilia went over and sat on the floor beside the girl and the dog. Cecilia thought of her own daughter, how she loved to run with Fury down the hill in the park, the child's gazelle stride and the dog's merry leaps.

'He's so soft,' the girl said. 'He must have cost a lot of money.'

'Actually, he's a rescue dog. We found him at a dog shelter.'

'Who could throw away a dog like this?'

'He was rambunctious. You should have seen.'

'I would never throw you away,' she said, putting her arms around the dog's neck. 'No matter how bad you were.'

'Fury was transferred from a sister shelter in the country. Normally, when the dogs arrive after travelling for hours in a crate, they're all frazzled and skittish. But Fury here trotted out with his tail wagging as if to say: Here I am! What's next?'

'I like that,' the girl said, stroking the dog. 'Here I am. What's next?'

Fury put his chin on her ankle and closed his eyes.

'I'm getting out tomorrow,' the girl said in a whisper.

'Really?' Cecilia said. 'That's great.'

'I think Tinker Bell needs help,' she said.

'Maybe,' Cecilia said.

'He wants to be good; he just doesn't know how.'

'Dogs can learn.'

'Maybe.' She looked at the wall where a window ought to be. There was none. 'I wish my mother's boyfriend didn't live with us. I wish he didn't live, full stop.'

Cecilia nodded.

'Sometimes I feel like it's me or him. Like perhaps I should just move out. Me and Tinky.'

Volunteers were discouraged from commenting on the patients' lives. The dog was a certified therapist, but Cecilia was not.

'You'll know what to do,' Cecilia said. 'You're smart.'

The girl looked down at Fury with a smile. 'I can just picture him being let out of his crate, all bouncy and cheerful.'

'Lunchtime,' the nurse called. 'Pet therapy's over.'

Cecilia looked at her watch. More than an hour had passed.

'Good luck tomorrow,' she said to the girl.

'You, too,' the girl said to her.

Dear Mrs Francis, Cecilia thought as she moved down the hall. Your son Tommy needs our help. He wants to be good, he just doesn't know how. Maybe if we take the time to sit down together . . .

It was a start.

Outside the hospital, Cecilia removed Fury's vest and gave him a biscuit. She imagined her kids at home as yet unpacked; her mother looking at her watch; the school reports; the density of her concerns blocking out the lithe summer day.

Twelve per cent, she thought.

Tomorrow the girl would walk out of these doors. Maybe she would sit on this bench for a moment and take in the lavender hedge that Cecilia had somehow failed to notice on the way in. The girl would notice. She was closer to one hundred per cent. Whether or not she could survive out here was an open question.

A breeze moved over the dog's coat and through Cecilia's hair. The scent of lavender was intoxicating. For a moment, Cecilia felt the ecstatic presence of the flowers, the actual joy that issued from them.

Fury gave a little tug on the leash. Here I am. He glanced at her. What's next?

A Remnant from the Past

BY MAVIS CHEEK

*E*lizabeth hid the invitation under the table and waited while Ian got ready to leave. As he turned away to button his overcoat she felt a rising irritation. It was Victorian, like covering up table legs, as if a man buttoning his overcoat were too vulgar for a woman to see. It's just a stupid remnant from the past, she thought, but she knew perfectly well that it was not the buttoning she found irritating. It was the fact that he was there at all, in the way of her opening the envelope.

'See you tonight,' he called from the hallway, and she called back that she would.

The front door clicked shut and he was gone. Only then did she realise that she had been holding her breath.

The card was deckle-edged with the faintest hint of gold and the writing semi-embossed in clear black. She would not expect it to be anything less than perfect. In the corner, neatly printed in his handwriting, was the name 'Betha'. And then, added in another hand, the words 'and Ian'.

She knew at once what had happened. He had forgotten Ian's name and his – wife? partner? secretary? – had added it later. That made her smile.

Pondering over his every word took her back more than twenty years, when she had almost made a religion out of it. Every syllable he spoke, every word he wrote, she had analysed for clues, meaning, hope. And now here she was, married, with two teenage children, and she was still doing it.

She ran her thumb over the bold, black lettering: *David Charles requests the pleasure of your company at his fiftieth birthday party to be held on . . .*

No one called her Betha now. That was another remnant from the past. She was Elizabeth. She smiled. A name that sounded older, wiser. But was she?

She ran into the kitchen, flicked the calendar to June and saw with relief that they were free. She wrote their acceptance immediately, addressing it to Harmony Brown, presumably at his office. She decided not to dwell on who Ms Brown might be. She was not going to allow anything more than mild curiosity to enter her head – or her heart.

'That was long ago and far away,' she told the muesli as she put it back in the cupboard. And that's that.

On the way to work she dropped the properly stamped envelope into the box. Only then did she realise she was breathing evenly again. They were going. It was fine.

But what should she wear? Whatever she chose would be wrong. Then she thought of Miranda and wondered if she would be there. Was she still as beautiful and elegant as ever? She had married a diplomat, she thought. Lived in – Egypt, was it? Somewhere like that. But probably they moved around all over the place; the exotic would always follow the exotic.

Suddenly it seemed pointless to worry about her clothes. Miranda would be there and Miranda would outshine her. Always had, always would.

In the end, she managed to forget all about frocks, shoes and posh parties, and concentrate on her work. But only just.

When Ian arrived home that evening she handed him the invitation and said, with admirable ease, 'Good, isn't it?'

He turned it over as if expecting something to be written on the back. 'Well, yes,' he said. 'But who's David Charles?'

Who indeed?

When Elizabeth first met him he was a fair Adonis, a few years out of Oxford and making money in the art world. He needed an assistant for his newly opened gallery and that was how it happened. From the first he called her Betha, and from the first she loved him secretly and silently. They worked well together, laughed a lot, and made a good and efficient team. She kept her eyes on the art sales, the business did well, he was grateful. He played hard, had many girlfriends, was known as a flirt (or worse) but there was no one serious.

Quite often, two or three times a month, they had

dinner together, and once he kissed her in a taxi – but that was after they had celebrated signing up Tom Marsh, who did that rare thing in those days of conceptual art – made good paintings – and much champagne had flowed. Still, the look he gave her that night stayed with her and she began to dare to hope . . .

Tom was an old friend whom David had tried for years to persuade to sign with him. It was a great coup and put the gallery on an international footing. It was through Tom that David met Miranda.

Elizabeth winced now to remember the contrast between herself and Miranda who was tall, slender, wore boots that came right up to her shapely thighs and little designer jackets that looked perfect. Miranda had style – and no serious man (the only similarity she shared with Betha). She invited Betha out to lunch and, without embarrassment, laid her cards on the table, for it never crossed her mind that there could be any romantic connection between David and his assistant. Clever, seductive Miranda was going to hold out for a whole lot more than a quick fling. Betha, looking into those beautiful eyes, went back to the gallery heavy of heart – and waited.

The battle began. Miranda would arrive at the gallery for lunch with David, or just for a chat, or occasionally they would go to the theatre or dinner; she would manage to be completely gorgeous – but always go home alone at night. David was suitably dazzled. Miranda, though keener than ever, as she told Betha, would not give in. They seemed locked in a battle of wills.

And then, one evening Miranda and David were invited to Tom's house for dinner, and Betha was not. That was the night it kicked off. Miranda sashayed in the following morning, her arm hooked through David's – and she winked at Betha. Disconcertingly, David also winked at her.

Their affair lasted for about three months until, one day, when Miranda rang for David he put his finger to his lips and shook his head. So it seemed it was just a fling after all. He went off to New York and Miranda arrived at the gallery looking slightly less than perfect. They had been told not to tell her David's whereabouts under any circumstances. Miranda fumed while David stayed away, setting up a gallery in Park Avenue. Miranda visited the London gallery often. By now she knew David was in New York, of course.

'You know what?' she said to Betha. 'He loved me too much anyway. He just couldn't handle it.'

Betha nodded and agreed that was very probably true.

When he returned he took Miranda out to a valedictory lunch, mopped up her tears and announced he was going to base himself in New York. Would Betha come too? Refusing very nearly broke her heart but she knew what she required, and it was not to be far from home, in a new country, watching him wade his way through other women. She declined. He was gratifyingly upset, amazed even, that she should refuse his offer, but Betha knew it was best. One more blow to the heart and she might not survive.

She remained in London, found a replacement at the gallery and left the world of art to join a bank. Easy, dull, anonymous. What she needed.

Miranda came to see her once more.

'I know I must have broken his heart,' she said. 'Poor David.'

Betha saw through the bravado. Miranda might act uncaring, but her face showed both misery and disappointment.

'Why,' Betha asked, 'did you ever give in?'

'Because, dear girl,' said Miranda archly, 'when we went to Tom's for dinner and I was upstairs in the bathroom, I heard David saying how much he wanted me, how deeply he was falling for me, how certain he was. He'd said it to my face loads of times, of course, but I'd never believed him. Then, overhearing it, well, I knew.'

Betha smiled, she hoped, sympathetically.

Miranda put her head on one side and asked, 'Didn't you ever fancy him? I bet you did. It must have been hard never having the chance.'

'Not at all,' she said. 'I just wanted him to be happy.'

'Most commendable,' said Miranda snappishly.

They left the restaurant and went their separate ways.

David rang Elizabeth once or twice and they had lunch a couple of times but he was mostly in New York.

She never asked him why he had stopped caring for Miranda. She was not much interested.

Everything moved on. He did not come to her wedding but sent them a lovely little Tom Marsh etching. When they moved she sent a change of address but they did not meet again and she settled him in the past. Or so she thought. But now here she was, getting excited again, ignoring her husband's raised eyebrow when she poured a second glass of wine with supper.

The next day, her feet back on the ground, she bought a little black frock. It was sensible.

At the crowded party, while Ian was happily talking to a man who collected old cars, she slipped away to speak to Tom.

'You look just the same,' he said.

'Nonsense.' She smiled. But she felt pleased at the gallantry. 'I haven't seen David yet,' she said, peering around.

Tom pointed him out. Elizabeth was shocked. It was, and was not, David. It was a semblance of Adonis, but one with thinning hair and a face more lined than lively. Slightly debauched looking, she thought. On the way here she had pictured him being the same as ever.

'Oh,' she said. And then, quickly, 'He's not as I thought.'

Tom laughed. 'Not aged well, has he? Never had the care of a good woman. And do you see who's trying to get next to him?'

'Miranda,' she said. 'Looking wonderful.'

'Yes, Miranda. Still after him, do you think?'

It certainly seemed that way.

Just then Miranda looked up and gave a little wave but she did not move from David's side.

'Maybe she'll be lucky this time?' she said, half to herself.

Tom laughed. 'Not a hope. I don't know why he bothered in the first place. Pride, I suppose. They were both determined. He to have a fling and—'

'She to marry him,' said Elizabeth.

'Do you remember my house in Fulham?' he said.

She looked surprised. 'Vaguely,' she said.

'Do you remember the bathroom? Upstairs?'

She shook her head. 'Why?'

'Because that's how he set the whole thing up. Like a game. He waited for her to go up there and then we stood below in the kitchen and he made out he was dying of desire. You could hear every word in that bathroom. And it worked. Well, for a short time.'

'That's horrible,' she said.

'David was not very nice where women were concerned. Except with you.'

'Me! He hardly knew I existed.'

'He knew very well you existed. He really liked you. He'd never have hurt you. He said so. You were probably the only woman under forty he didn't try it on with.'

Tom laughed at her shocked face. That bit was true, at least, she thought.

At the sound of Tom's laugh, David looked up with an expression of surprise – and then smiled broadly. He came towards them with Miranda hot on his heels.

Elizabeth turned. There was Ian, now standing alone, looking a little forlorn. She ran to him, bumping through the crowd, and she hooked her hand through his arm. Then, with her husband by her side, she returned to David, Miranda and Tom, her face radiant.

Or so she was told by her host as he kissed her cheek and added, 'Betha – I'm so glad you came.'

And she, replying, said, 'Thank you. So am I. And David, this is my husband. His name is Ian.'

The Ammonite

BY TRACY CHEVALIER

*R*obert couldn't believe it when he saw it lying on the sand in front of him, close enough that he could have spat on it. Yet it might as well have been on another beach in another country, for he could not get out of his wheelchair, or even bend over, to pick it up.

Ammonites were not usually found on this sandy part of the beach, but further along the shore, where it was rockier and the cliffs exposed the Jurassic limestone that held so many fossils. He longed to handle the ammonite, to feel its cold, hard ridges bite into his palm, the round, spiral shape a familiar comfort in his hand. During his long career as a geologist, Robert had found hundreds of ammonites, yet still felt that childlike thrill at discovering another.

Not far from him a small boy was trying to build a sandcastle in sand that was too soft to hold its shape. Again and again he filled his bucket and up-ended it, only for the sand to collapse in a heap. You should be down by the water's edge, Robert wanted to say, where the sand is firm. Why doesn't his mother tell him, instead of lying there, asleep? I would, if I could.

'Agnes!' he shouted.

From behind him came her disembodied voice. 'What you want, Robert?' He could feel her leaning against the wheelchair's handles.

'Ammonite,' he said.

'What?'

'Ammo—' Robert ran out of breath.

Agnes came into view. 'What is it now, old man?'

Although she had been looking after him for a year, Robert was always stunned by her appearance. Agnes's skin was as dark as his mahogany dining table. She had round black eyes, a wide mouth and a loud laugh. Her hair was magnificent and terrifying, especially whenever she came back from a break in London, where she had it done. Sometimes it was in elaborate braids that wound around her head like fine ropes. Other times she had it straightened and occasionally dyed a rust colour, or once – disastrously, Robert thought – streaked with blonde highlights. Sometimes he didn't recognise her when she came back and it sent him into a panic to think that she had been replaced by another stranger.

'Ammo—' he repeated.

' "Am I" what? Am I in Lyme Regis, like I been pestering Agnes for so long to come? Yes, old man, you in Lyme Regis. You happy at last?'

Agnes stepped in front of him, treading on the

ammonite as she tucked a plaid blanket tighter around Robert's legs.

'No!' Robert cried, worried the ammonite would get buried in the sand.

Agnes clucked her tongue in her cheek.

'I bring you all the way here and you can't even pretend you happy? What I going to do with you?'

'That's—'

That's not what I mean. Let me explain. Look at that ammonite. It is 180 million years old.

There were so many things Robert wanted to say, so many words that got stuck somewhere between his brain and his tongue. I miss my wife. When will my son come back from Bahrain to visit? My back itches. It's hell no longer being able to speak properly. I'm sorry. Thank you for everything you do for me. I am so grateful. I am so frightened.

Robert and his wife and son had often come here to hunt for fossils, following in the footsteps of the great nineteenth-century fossil hunters. They combed the mile-long shore between Lyme Regis and Charmouth for thin cylinders of belemnites; for pointed half-shells of bivalves nicknamed the Devil's toenails; for the elegant ribbed spirals of ammonites. Occasionally they found parts of ichthyosaurs and plesiosaurs, the enormous pre-dinosaur fossils the beach was famous for. Robert had always hoped he might find a complete ichthyosaur, but had had to content himself with vertebrae, ribs and jaw fragments.

It was just one of many things Robert had realised

he would not achieve in his life. For instance, he had hoped to move to Lyme Regis with his wife after his retirement, but she had died before they could manage it. Coming to visit was perhaps a mistake, the town mocking him with its fossils now beyond his reach.

Agnes reached over and smoothed down his hair, which the sea breeze had ruffled.

'You want an ice cream, old man? I know you like it.'

She did not wait for Robert to try to reply, but disappeared behind him.

'Don't go anywhere!' he heard her add, followed by her raucous laugh.

He looked down. Half of the ammonite was poking out of the sand. You can't get me, old man, it was saying.

'Agnes!' he shouted.

Agnes ignored his cry. She had learned to ignore many of Robert's cries now, for he shouted out her name incessantly. Sometimes she thought she would go insane from hearing her name so much.

When she first started to work for Robert, he had been better: wheelchair-bound, but able to hold a conversation. He had complained a great deal, which had irritated Agnes. If he had grown up in South Africa as she had, with poverty and violence underpinning every aspect of life, he would not complain, but would appreciate his solid, spacious home and his money.

Now, though, she missed his complaints. At least they had been part of a two-way conversation. These days he couldn't complete a sentence, and Agnes had to guess at what he meant and anticipate what he might want or need.

She walked along the seafront, the lone black face among the crowds of holidaymakers. It had taken her a long time to let go of her anxiety at being with so many white people. She had never actually experienced outright racism in Dorset; it was more surprised looks quickly concealed, followed by curious sideways glances. She had never felt threatened, but it was still a relief to get to London and her cousin's flat, surrounded by black skin and the smell of hot hair oil, the taste of mutton and rice, and the sound of Xhosa, her own language. Only then could she truly relax.

At the ice cream stand she asked for two 99s with Flakes, and waited for them with her eyes closed, her face turned towards the sun. It had been an unusually hot, bright summer, which meant that the neighbours in Robert's village complained about the heat. They also complained when it was cold or rainy; there seemed to be no pleasing the English. Agnes had never met people so obsessed with the weather.

When she first came to the village the women had all looked the same to her, with names that sounded so similar, she mixed them up: Pam and Pat, Jane and Jean, Sue and Prue. It took her months to tell them apart, and to trust them.

They had been kind to her, but sometimes Agnes wondered how they would respond when she woke one morning and found that Robert had passed away in the night. For he would. It was only a matter of time. And she knew she would want to run out into the road and throw her arms over her head and wail, as she had done when her husband had died. None of the women here had ever raised their voices, even when one lost her own husband. That funeral had been so hushed, as was the reception at the house after. Agnes had heard just a sniffle here and there, and seen tears in eyes that never spilled over. Grief here was expressed so differently.

When the man handed Agnes her ice creams, she turned automatically to hand them to her son and daughter, and felt a sharp pang. They were not there, of course, but in South Africa with her mother. When Agnes's husband had died two years earlier, she had decided to come to England, sending back more money in a month than she could save in six months at home. That was one of the few things she had in common with Robert: their children were far away.

The ice creams were already melting in the sun, sending white tears down her dark hands. She licked them away as she headed back to Robert. A crowd had gathered around the wheelchair, and it took her a moment to realise it was empty. Agnes dropped the ice creams, which landed with plops in the sand, the cones sticking up like horns.

'Robert!' she cried, the beginning of the wail she had been rehearsing rising in her throat.

Simon looked up from his latest failed sandcastle just in time to see the man fall from his chair on wheels.

Simon had studied the chair when it first appeared next to him on the beach. Only the dark skin of the woman pushing it had interested him as much.

There were certainly a lot of curious things to look at out here. Simon's mother had promised him they might even see the bones of a dinosaur at the beach. They had looked, but found only a funny round thing with stripes on it that reminded Simon of some buttons on one of his mother's dresses. His mother had called it something, but Simon couldn't remember what. Also, he seemed to have lost it, for it was no longer in the pocket of his swimming trunks. Maybe he could find another later when they looked for dinosaurs again.

Simon wondered if his father would be better at finding dinosaurs. However, this wasn't his weekend to see Simon.

The man hit the ground with a noise that sounded like his mother slumping into the sofa after a long game of sword-fighting with Simon. The man didn't move for a moment, but then he reached out to grab at something in the sand. Curious, Simon dropped his bucket and crawled over to see what he had found, pushing his way through the grown-ups who had gathered around the chair and were discussing what to do.

Then the woman with the dark skin was there, yelling, 'Robert!'

Simon smiled and looked around. Robert was his father's name. But his father wasn't there – only his mother, who had been asleep in the sand and was now rolling over.

The dark lady squatted by the fallen man. 'Oh Lord, Robert, you all right?'

'Ammonite,' Robert said.

The dark lady stared at him. 'Ammonite? How is it you say that so clearly, old man?'

The man held out his hand to Simon. The striped button rested on his palm. 'Ammonite,' he repeated.

'Oh!' Simon cried. 'You found it! My ammonite.' He reached for it, then paused. 'You can have it. I'll find another. Would you like to keep it?'

Simon's mother sat up. 'Simon? What's wrong?'

'Nothing's wrong. Robert's got my ammonite. I've given it to him.'

'No, no, little boy, you take back your stone,' the dark lady said. 'Robert, give the boy back his stone!'

The man closed his hand around the ammonite.

'It's not a stone, it's a fossil,' Simon said. 'It's an ammonite.'

Robert looked at Simon. 'Thank you.'

'That's all right,' Simon replied. 'Will you help me find a dinosaur now?'

'Yes,' Robert said. 'Yes, I will.'

Grit in My Eye

BY LEE CHILD

I told the television people I wanted my wife there during the interview. It wasn't what they had in mind. They wanted to film me in a darkened room, alone, with dramatic lighting. I said we needed to send a different message. I said we needed a bright sunny room, with my wife sitting next to me, to show that old secrets could be brought out into the daylight now, and that public witnesses could hear them. I said the imagery and the symbolism were important.

They agreed, as I knew they would, because it was a good argument. Not quite true, though.

My real reason was memory. All these things happened thirty years ago, and I was afraid of forgetting some of the details. Nothing important, but a name or two might slip away from me, and I didn't want to look like an idiot. I didn't want the viewers to think I had taken one too many blows to the head, in the service of my country. So I wanted my wife there, because she knows it all too, and she could help me.

So the film crew set up in our living room and we clipped tiny microphones to our clothes. The interviewer

49

was a serious man, because the programme was a serious documentary. It was going to be a contribution to history, to posterity, so I was expecting serious questions. But the first one was relatively gentle. An introduction, really. Not even a question, actually, but a statement.

The interviewer said, 'You're the only man alive who knows the true story of the spy who used the name Tony Jackson.'

I said, 'Yes.'

He said, 'You wrote a book about him.'

I said, 'Yes,' because I had, a quarter of a century ago.

The first line went, 'It started with grit in his eye, and it ended with three dead.' Which was a good first line, I thought. It grabbed the reader's attention.

The book had done well. Some of it was even true, but it was limited to the period in question, which was six days in Moscow. People forget what Moscow was like thirty years ago. It was still a savage battleground back then. The Cold War was still far from over. Which was why we sent people like the man who used the name Tony Jackson.

His story started long before he got there, of course, and it continued long after he left. The six days between the grit in his eye and the three dead Russians was only a small part of it.

The interviewer asked, 'What kind of a man was Tony Jackson?'

Which was the first tough question. Because Tony

Jackson was two things. In the here-and-now, he was everything you would expect from a modern secret agent. He was superbly fit and strong, of course, and highly educated, and even something of an intellectual. People without brains just can't do this kind of work. He was also civilised, and urbane, and he had sophisticated hobbies and interests.

But in another sense he stretched all the way back to the Stone Age. All people do, really, because we are all the product of slow evolution. We all carry traces of an ancient, brutal past. But the doors in Tony Jackson's DNA were all standing wide open. He could reach back and still be a caveman. He refused to be beaten. You had to know two things about him: whoever you were, he was smarter than you, and he was more ruthless than you. If you challenged him, he would beat you. He would find a way.

Except he didn't, that time in Moscow.

He was sent over in the very late 1970s. The Soviets had just invaded Afghanistan, and the Americans had announced they were pulling out of the Olympics. Tension was high and spying was big business. Tony went as part of a sophisticated machine, with some amazing infrastructure. We had microphones everywhere and hundreds of informants. We had even dug a secret tunnel under the KGB's private telephone exchange, to tap their calls. We knew all their agents.

There was so much raw information to process, we started a brand-new system. We listed all their operatives and gave each one a shadow, an agent of our own whose only job was to track their target's every move, every minute of every day, to live their target's life alongside them, really.

In their reports, they tended to say, 'I did this, and now I'm going to do that.' One person became two, in effect. It was a boom time for employment.

Then we realised the system wasn't new. And it wasn't even ours. The KGB had been using it for years. Each one of our agents had his own shadow. Even the shadows had shadows. It was a serious obstacle to efficiency. So the first task for any new agent was to identify his Soviet shadow and eliminate him. Standard practice, like a sort of operational throat-clearing. So Tony Jackson trained for five years, and arrived in Moscow, and set about hunting his shadow.

The interviewer asked, 'And what happened?'

He got grit in his eye, that's what happened. On his first day.

He was walking across Red Square, a little suspicious of a man in a raincoat who was walking behind him. Then a gust of swirling autumn wind came up, with all of Moscow's filth in it, and it lashed and battered at him, and suddenly he couldn't see anything, and tears were streaming down his face. He ground his knuckles in his eyes and turned around, but the man in the raincoat was gone. A failure, on his first day.

He wiped his eyes and one of them felt OK, but the other had a problem. He blinked and made faces and shook his head, but he couldn't fix it. He stumbled onward in the shadow of the Kremlin wall, and he bumped into a Russian woman who was trying to pass him by. He apologised, in character, in perfect Russian, and she smiled a small, embarrassed smile and moved on.

Then she turned back.

She was slender, for a Russian, and fair, and good-looking in an elfin way, but not especially young and not especially well. She looked tired, and washed out, and a little beaten down. Normal, in other words, for Moscow. She was dressed in a two-piece tweed suit at least ten years out of fashion, by Western standards, but it was neat and clean and it looked good on her.

She asked, 'Can I help you?'

Tony said, 'I've got something in my eye.'

She was shorter than him, so she stood close and looked up. She asked, 'May I?'

She reached up and used her finger and thumb to separate his eyelids. She took out a small linen hand-kerchief and tented it to a point and dabbed the point on her tongue.

'Hold still,' she said.

He stood still and she reached up very carefully. He watched her with his good eye. She was holding her breath and concentrating hard. Her lips were parted and the tip of her tongue was between her teeth. Her eyes were blue and she had fine lines in her skin. Her handkerchief smelled of lavender.

'Look up,' she said, and he did, although he didn't want to, because it meant looking at the leaden sky, not at her.

'Look left,' she said, and he did, at the top of the Kremlin's onion domes. She moved the damp point of the handkerchief, in and out, decisively, and she said, 'There.'

She backed away a step and he blinked and felt better and looked down at a small black speck on the linen. He felt suddenly lost and alone and stupid. Five years of training with one of the world's mightiest organisations, and the very first day of his very first mission had been blown, all because of a tiny fragment of Mother Russia, carried on the wind. He felt un-equal to his task. He wanted to go home. Normal, for Moscow. It was like another planet. The first day was always the most stressful.

He said, 'Thank you.'

She said, 'It was nothing.'

He said, 'Will you have dinner with me?'

She wore no wedding ring. He thought she must be a mid-level manager, maybe with a state department store. Not useful to him professionally, but that was a point in her favour.

She said, 'I don't know.'

'At my hotel,' he said. 'I just got here. I design tractor parts. I'm supposed to go to a meeting tomorrow.'

The interviewer asked me, 'Did she say yes?'

I looked into the camera and said, 'Yes, she said yes.'

But Tony wasn't sure she would go through with it. He took a table for two in the hotel dining room and waited. And she came in right on time, still wearing the tweed two-piece, but with a different blouse. She was good company. Shy, and reserved, but not excessively. Her name was Magda. She didn't say how old she was, but Tony guessed forty. She had never been married, but from references in her conversation he understood she had been in at least one long relationship. She was not a manager in a department store. She kept the books for a government printer, in a southern suburb.

They went to bed together that night, unable to resist, both of them lonely, she as a faceless cog in a giant machine, he as a man in great danger far from home. They went to bed together the next night too, and the next, and by their fourth night together Tony was pretty sure there was more than loneliness involved, on her part as well as his.

After their fifth night together, Tony was arrested.

Magda had left his room before dawn, so she was safe, presumably, but when he walked out to the street a little after nine, he was immediately set upon by a number of large men. Resistance was impossible. He was driven the short distance to the Lubyanka prison and locked in a cell. He was ashamed. At best he would be exchanged for a traitor or two held at home, and then he would live out his life as a failure. But he was terrified too, because at worst he wouldn't be exchanged, but sent to Siberia, or executed.

He was left alone with his thoughts for a whole day. Which was normal, for Moscow.

The interviewer asked, 'Then what happened?'

It got worse before it got better, that's what happened. His cell door opened and Magda walked in. She was wearing the same tweed two-piece. At first Tony thought she was a prisoner too, and he felt he had somehow involved her, or betrayed her, but then he realised that prisoners couldn't just flit from cell to cell on a whim.

Magda smiled and said, 'I'm your shadow, you idiot. I got you first.'

Tony was devastated, of course. Doubly so, in fact, because first he had made a huge professional error, and then he had fallen in love with his enemy.

But then something extraordinary happened. Magda bent down to where he lay on his bed and she kissed him. Then she took a small gun out of her pocket and slipped it to him.

She said, 'Listen carefully. You're regarded as very important. Therefore, they'll send their top three interrogators. I know of no other way to identify them. Shoot them, and then we'll get out together.'

All Tony could say was, 'Why?'

Magda answered, 'Because I love you, you idiot.'

The interviewer said, 'Hence the three dead Russians.'

I said, 'Yes.'

He said, 'Tony Jackson was a false name, wasn't it?'

I said, 'Yes.'

'It was you, wasn't it?'

I said, 'Yes.'

'And this is Magda, isn't it?'

Beside me, my wife of thirty years smiled and nodded.

A Night Out

BY HELEN DUNMORE

The green beast squatted in the sun, grinning at her. Ruth climbed back on the seat with the instruction booklet and went through it all again. Brake engaged, blades disengaged. Choke halfway out. For the fourth time, she turned the ignition key. For the fourth time the engine caught, vibrated and died.

Ruth's heart pounded with rage. She got off the mower, drew back her foot and kicked the green flank as hard as she could. Pulses of pain shot up her leg, but the mower wasn't even marked. Hot, choking fury filled her throat. Now she was pummelling the metal with her fists, yelling words that the beast would never have heard from Donald in a million years of mowing.

Her hands hurt. She wasn't shouting any more. She was crying, leaning against the beast, crying in huge, painful jags that had never come in all the six months since the funeral.

'Mrs Carver? Ruth!'

A face was peeping over the high fence. How had she got up there?

'If you want, I can help with your lawn tractor,' said Aruna Patel, as if she hadn't noticed tears, thuds or swearing.

'It's a ride-on mower,' said Ruth mechanically.

'I am very familiar with them. Wait one moment.'

The face disappeared. The Patels had been living next door for two years: a professional couple, always extremely busy, leaving for work at seven in the morning in expensive cars. The young man's widowed mother, Aruna, lived with them. Ruth and Donald had tried to be friendly, of course.

She was at the gate.

'It's very kind of you, Aruna.'

'Not at all.' Aruna was as businesslike today as her son.

Ruth stood aside. 'I know there's enough petrol in it,' she said, trying to sound competent.

'But not enough oil. There is a safety cut-out to protect against damage, if the oil level is low. See, the warning light is on.'

So it was.

'You seem to know a lot about these things. My husband – Donald – would never let me near it. He was like a child.'

'Devan is the same. Exactly the same. However, he is out all day and I like to know how things work.' She laughed, and Ruth found that she was smiling too. 'We have oil in the garage. I will get some for you.'

'Don't bother now. The grass can stay long for one more day.'

'But you have such a beautiful lawn. I have often admired it.'

'It would make a great campsite,' said Ruth, surveying it.

She had often thought that, but Donald would never let tents be pitched on his precious lawn. She'd thought that when they had grandchildren, he would change his mind. But Donald would never see his grandchildren.

'He was only fifty-eight,' she said, very quietly, as she had said it so often to herself.

'My husband also,' said Aruna. 'Heart attack. He was fifty-six.'

The two women were silent. The glossy green of the mower blurred as Ruth said, 'There were so many things we were going to do. I took early retirement—'

'We had the business. We could never go away together.'

It took them the rest of the day to mow the lawn. Aruna waved away Ruth's protests and once the oil was topped up the mower ran like a dream.

'Now your campsite is ready,' said Aruna.

The expanse of grass suddenly looked enormous to Ruth. Ridiculous, for just one woman. Why was she doing all this? Keeping on with everything? Everybody said you had to keep going. What for?

But then the smell of cut grass caught her so strongly that she felt dizzy. Why did it smell so sweet? It reminded her of Guide Camp. Blaise Fields had just been mowed when they had pitched their tents. Ruth had woken at dawn, clambered over the others without waking anybody and put her head out of the tent. Everything was grey and wet with dew. It smelled wonderful.

Aruna was staring at the golden tops of the trees, her eyes half closed. 'When I was a little girl,' she said, 'we had a most beautiful garden.'

'Did you grow up here, or in India?'

'Oh no, we lived in Uganda. Our house was a bungalow, with a big verandah running all around. On hot nights the servants would push my bed outside. I would wake up in the night and see the stars. I always preferred to be outside. Running and climbing and getting in the way of the garden boys.'

'I was a tomboy too. My own daughter was just the opposite. Everything had to be Barbie pink.'

'I know. It is like a disease. Mine was the same. But now she is living in Tasmania, so she has to be practical.'

'Lucy's in New York.'

The two women fell silent again, thinking of faraway, beloved daughters, and of the endless Skyping and emails that never quite filled the gaps.

'I must be going home,' said Aruna briskly.

'I've still got the tent,' said Ruth, as if to herself.

Aruna's expression sharpened. 'Have you? How big is it?'

'It's a two-man tent. Donald and I – but that was years ago. I expect it's fallen to pieces.'

'You could look, perhaps?'

*

Next morning, Ruth looked. Dear, careful Donald had rolled it away immaculately, as if it was never to be used again. It was a very low-tech tent. Ruth remembered how she used to wrestle with its poles and guy-ropes.

She came to a decision. I'll put it up, she thought, just to see how it looks.

The sun was hot on Ruth's back as she hammered in the last tent-peg. The cream canvas was spotted with age and damp, but the fabric remained strong. She inched her way inside. It was very warm. A blackbird ran across the angle of her vision, a few feet away. She'd forgotten how close birds came, when you were camping. She would make a cup of tea, bring it out and watch them.

As Ruth emerged from the tent, she heard the clip of secateurs. Instantly, she knew that Aruna was in her garden, too. Aruna would have heard the hammering. But she would not come into Ruth's garden, unless Ruth asked.

I could sit in the sun with my tea, Ruth thought. She was getting used to being on her own. Make the tea, perhaps with a couple of biscuits, wash it up, think about cooking, decide a boiled egg will do, email Lucy, save it as a draft because emailing every day is too needy, think about joining a book group, decide to leave it until the autumn, see what's on TV—

'Aruna?' called Ruth. 'Aruna, are you there?'

Seconds later, Aruna's head popped over the fence.

'How do you get up so high?' asked Ruth.

'I have steps for trimming the hedges.' Aruna's eyes brightened and widened. 'My goodness. I see that you know what you are doing when it comes to tents.'

'It's old-fashioned, but quite roomy inside. Come and have a look.'

Aruna's sari did not seem to get in her way as she crawled into the tent and then twisted herself into a sitting position. Her gold bangles chinked as she waved her hand admiringly. 'There is so much space! You would not believe it from the outside.'

'I'm going to sleep out in it,' said Ruth suddenly.

'Alone?'

'I'll be perfectly all right in my own garden,' said Ruth.

'Of course,' said Aruna, looking away, her voice suddenly distant, and Ruth realised once again that Aruna would never – not without being asked –

'Although I would feel much more secure if I camped with someone else.'

'That is very natural,' said Aruna.

'And I wondered if perhaps— You did say you liked sleeping out?'

'You mean that I should camp here?' asked Aruna, and her voice sounded so surprised that Ruth wondered if, in some way she didn't understand, she had offended her neighbour.

'Well, yes. But it was only an idea. Probably not a very good one—'

'And see the stars . . .' said Aruna dreamily.

'Well, maybe not through the canvas. It's quite thick.'

'I will peep out of the tent-flaps in the dead of night.'

'I'll buy those blow-up camping mattresses. Alex says they're wonderful.'

'No, please! Allow me!'

They wrangled gently over mattresses, a camping stove and sleeping bags. They made lists and discussed timings. Aruna learned the route to Ruth's downstairs cloakroom. It became clear that Aruna's son and daughter-in-law were to know nothing.

'I will simply slip back into the house when morning comes.'

And here they were, side by side in sleeping bags, with the tent-flaps open to the warm night.

Aruna wrote in her diary in the fading light. 'Just two sentences. I began it years ago to practise my English.'

How strongly the garden smelled of earth and falling dew, of cut grass, flowers and the distant compost heap. Ruth lay on her back and watched an ant on its slow journey across the pale curve of the tent. The light was nearly gone . . .

She woke, because Aruna had fallen on top of her.

'I am so sorry! So sorry! I lost my way to your cloakroom and there was a fox or some night animal running across the grass so I hurried into the tent rather quickly—'

Ruth could not help it: the vision of Aruna scrambling into the tent pursued by a night animal was too much for her. She laughed until she had to roll on her side to ease the pain in her stomach. Thank heavens, Aruna was laughing too.

They didn't go back to sleep.

'It's a beautiful night, full of stars,' said Aruna, and turned her sleeping bag round so she could lie on her back and watch them through the tent-flaps.

They talked as the grey of dawn took away the starlight, and while the sun rose, creating unfamiliar shadows across the lawn. They talked about Donald and Manu, about Lucy and Jyoti, about time-zones and funerals, about daughters-in-law and tree-climbing. Their voices rose and fell as the birds woke and took over the garden with their song.

It was Ruth who heard the click of the gate. She sat up, her skin prickling. Much too early for the postman or deliveries—

It was the young man from next door, walking across the grass. He saw Ruth peering out of her tent and asked politely, 'Excuse me, have you seen my mother?'

'It is my Devan,' said Aruna. She wriggled out her sleeping bag and stood to face her son.

'Mother!'

'What is it?'

'I woke up and your bed was empty. I thought something had happened to you, and then I heard all this talking and laughing.'

'So you came to investigate,' said Ruth.

66

'But Mother . . .'

The young man's arm swept out to indicate the tent, the garden, the sleeping bag and his mother with her long plait over her shoulder.

'What are you doing here? Why are you not at home in your bed?'

He looks so bewildered, thought Ruth. Like a little boy.

Aruna must have seen it too, for she said soothingly, 'I will come home, Devan. I will come now. The night is over.'

Hastily Aruna gathered her things, nodding at Ruth as if to reassure her, too. 'I will come later and help you to take down the tent,' she promised.

'I might keep it up,' said Ruth.

She watched them walk away, mother and son. It had only been one night, after all. He had nothing to worry about.

It was when Ruth was shaking the sleeping bags that Aruna's diary fell out and lay open on the grass. You must never read people's private diaries, but as Ruth bent over to pick it up she could not help seeing the two lines:

'I am camping in a tent with my friend Ruth. We are hoping to see the stars.'

The Promotion

BY JANE FALLON

I never asked to be promoted.

Actually, that's not true. I did. Regularly. Twice a year at my biannual appraisal. Of course I did, everyone did. It was just something to say to fill the time between 'Your timekeeping could be better' and 'You're not due a pay review until August'. And they seemed to like it if you showed a bit of ambition.

And then, when Julie my line manager upped and left to become a full-time mum, she suggested that I apply for her job. I was highly thought of, she said, and the heads of department liked me. I decided it made sense. Just to show willing. I didn't actually want the job, though. Or, at least, I thought I didn't.

Angie, my best friend both in and out of work, my partner in too many crimes to mention, helped me fill out the form. We fell about laughing as I tried to remember all the white lies and embellishments I had put on my original CV three and a half years ago so that I could replicate them. In the end we just made up some new ones.

When I got to 'Why do you want this position?' and

I struggled to come up with a response, Angie said I should just put, 'I don't, I just thought I should be seen to apply,' which was tempting.

In the end, I settled for something generic, something that sounded good without really meaning anything, something that they would have read on a hundred application forms before mine. I asked Angie to read it through, which she did, and she declared it 'absolutely fine', and then it was five-thirty so we headed to the White Hart and had a big glass of wine, as we did most days. In the pub, we laughed about how ridiculous it would be if I got an interview, and how awful an outcome if I became her boss.

Once I had handed in the application, though, once it was too late to go back and change anything, I started to wonder: what would be so bad about being promoted?

Angie and I had always agreed that we would never want to be management. You had to take work too seriously. Being one of the staff could be fun; you were all in it together, united in your scorn for your superiors and your disdain for your job. Being a boss always seemed so . . . lonely, so grown-up.

But stumbling home to my tiny flat after yet another glass of wine too many with Angie in the pub, clutching my Indian takeaway and trying to think of yet another excuse to avoid having to sit and watch TV alone, it occurred to me that maybe it was time for me to become a grown-up myself. After years of my being the working single mum whose job was way down the

list of her priorities, behind helping with the homework and attending sports day, my daughter Ellen had
left to go to university and I had embarked on a second
youth, spending most evenings down the pub, moan-
ing about work and with no real plan of how the future
was going to go. Things had to change.

Next day, I told Angie how I was feeling. I tell
her everything. We met on my first day in the accounts department of Beadle, McAlpine, Hogarth – a
middling-sized marketing company – and we've been
inseparable ever since. She had the desk opposite me
and at lunchtime she took me round to the best local
sandwich shop and gave me the lowdown on all my
new colleagues. She had already worked there for
eighteen months so she pretty much had everyone
sized up. She told me who to avoid and who was a
pushover and which of the blokes was most likely to try
it on at the annual Christmas party. We quickly
became firm friends both in and out of the office.

At that time there was a thriving social life attached
to work. As the years went on, I barely noticed that all
around us our colleagues were sobering up and settling
down, going on maternity leave and rising up the
career ladder, until it was just Angie and me, hell-bent
on having a good time. Except that now, suddenly, our
late nights felt a bit forced, a bit desperate.

Angie couldn't believe I was serious when I told her
I was going to ask for my application form back, to
plead for twenty-four more hours before I would have
to resubmit it. Did I seriously want to become one of

them, she asked me. What about the longer hours and the fact that I would never be able to skive off just because I wanted a few more hours in bed ever again? I told her I didn't care.

I knew that if I got the job it would change the dynamics of our friendship for ever. Angie wasn't easy to manage at the best of times. She had a strong 'us and them' work ethic that had rubbed off on me early on. But the idea of her having to report to me, her friend – well, let's just say it wasn't easy to imagine. I couldn't picture my life without her in it as my best friend, but I'd discovered that I couldn't picture it continuing as it was, either.

So I stuck to my guns, retrieved my application form and set about filling out a new one. I called Ellen for moral support.

'About time,' she said. 'I wondered when you would discover your inner ambition.' Ellen has finished her degree and is now at law school, by the way. No young single motherhood for her.

Angie was on her best behaviour the next day. She couldn't quite bring herself to wish me luck, but she did ask to look over my form again and she made a few suggestions, which is the closest she'll ever come to saying 'I'm sorry.' I changed a couple of things, handed it in to Clare in Human Resources and endeavoured to forget all about it.

That night, back in the White Hart, she said wistfully, 'I don't suppose we'll do this any more if you get the job.'

'Of course we will,' I said. 'Just not every night.'

'It'll be different, though,' she said, and she looked so miserable that I felt awful, as if I was letting her down.

I started to wish I had just taken my form back and not resubmitted it. Since Ellen left home, I don't know what I would have done without Angie. Did I really want to jeopardise our friendship? I tried to talk it over with her, but she just shrugged and said I should do whatever I wanted.

Once, when she'd had a couple more Pinot Grigios than usual, Angie had confided in me that all she really wanted was to meet the right man and have a baby. OK, so I had failed spectacularly on the man front, but did I know how lucky I was to have Ellen?

I told her I did. Ellen was unequivocally the best thing that had ever happened to me. Angie told me tearfully that she had all but given up meeting someone she liked enough to have a child with before it was too late. I felt desperately sorry for her, but the next day it was as if she had forgotten she had ever confided in me. She had her 'couldn't care less' face back on. That's the thing about Angie, she doesn't like to show any vulnerability. Ever.

Three or so days later, I heard I had an interview. I was almost scared to tell Angie, but she smiled and said that she wished me good luck. I agonised about what to wear and I let her convince me that I should dress the same way as I always do. These people knew me already. If I came in dressed up to the nines one day, it would just draw attention to the fact that I ordinarily looked a little less groomed. Still, it took me an hour to get ready in the morning, trying on five different outfits before I decided that the first one was the best.

I felt stupidly nervous and I made Angie spend the morning helping me practise my answers to the questions I thought they might ask me. She was looking pretty smart herself as well, I noticed, which usually meant she had a date, although I knew by now not to ask. I would find out later anyway because, if she didn't already have plans, I knew she would want a full debrief in the White Hart after work.

The interview went as well as I could have hoped. At one point they asked me what I thought of Angie and how we worked together. It worried me that they were clearly thinking she would make it difficult for me if I got promoted, so, even though I knew they were probably right, I went out of my way to defend her and to let them know how talented she really is. Which, actually, is the truth. She has an incredibly quick brain and a natural attention to detail that is a godsend in accounting. I felt so guilty that my applying for the job might have made them see her in a more negative light that I went completely over the top, singing her praises and insisting that she and I had such a strong working relationship that a change of status for one of us couldn't ever harm it.

Days passed and I found my nerves escalating. I veered wildly between wanting the job and hoping they didn't offer it to me. I was so scared that, whatever I had said in my interview, Angie and my friendship wouldn't survive my being promoted. But Ellen was so convinced I was going to get the job that after a while her confidence started to rub off on me and I dared to start imagining myself in my new role. I could picture a new professional me striding into the future. A woman with a career, not just a job. I convinced myself that I could make it work with Angie. It might be tricky at first, but she'd soon see it hadn't changed me.

I waited.

Then one day I got to work to find Angie grinning like a Cheshire cat.

'What's up with you?' I said, reflecting her smile. Maybe she'd met the man of her dreams after all.

'I don't know how to tell you this,' she said. 'But I got the job.'

I was momentarily confused. 'What job?'

'The job here. Julie's job.'

'I don't understand,' I said. 'I didn't even know you'd applied . . .'

All those days I'd talked it over with her, worrying about what to say on my application form, practising my answers before the interview. All those nights when I'd agonised over whether my being promoted would get in the way of our friendship. Angie had never expressed an interest in the job. She'd never once hinted she might apply.

'Why didn't you say anything?'

Her smile never wavered. 'Because you were my competition.'

I didn't know what to say. This was my best friend, or that's what I thought.

'Aren't you going to congratulate me?'

She was already clearing her desk, ready for the big move into the office up the corridor.

'It's going to be strange, me being your boss,' she said, not really looking as if she was worried by it. 'Obviously things'll have to change. I'll be working later hours and I can't really be drinking down the pub every night.'

'Of course. Congratulations . . .' I started to say, but she'd already left, belongings in a big box, heading off for her new life. She didn't look back.

Breakfast with Mr Gillyflower

BY KATIE FFORDE

*H*annah's move to the country was working brilliantly. She'd always wanted to move out of the town and live surrounded by fields and woodland, with stunning views. And she saw no reason why she should wait until she was of retirement age to have her dream. The property boom was also a factor. She sold her house in Bristol at the top of the market and bought a tiny, but adorable, cottage – also at the top of the market – in the Cotswolds. She had spare cash with which to do it up from the sale of her Bristol house and she loved her new life. So far, she hadn't had time to be lonely.

She set up a little workspace so she could gaze at hills that gradually became greener as the year edged out of winter into spring. The Severn snaked its silver way to the Bristol Channel and lambs appeared on the hill. Every day she felt joy in her new surroundings, glad that she'd ignored her city friends' negative opinions about turning bucolic so young, their worries about her having no companions her own age.

'There's a cottage being done up just near me,' she

told them. 'A lovely family might move in. The woman and I will start a book group.'

Although she had been joking, the village did have a lot more to offer than many. It wasn't only filled with commuters and retired people. There were many young families and a few newly-weds. She hadn't come across many single people in her age group, but there was a good friendly pub and a thriving shop with a post office. There was even a hairdresser's, which, although more accustomed to traditional wash-and-sets and perms, could do a passable cut-and-blow-dry and keep Hannah in reasonable shape in between visits to her old hairdresser.

When her work was done or if she needed a break, she climbed the hill so she could see beyond the Severn to Wales. Although she couldn't decide if she was looking at the Brecon Beacons or the Black Mountains, she could pick out the Sugar Loaf and was thrilled to be able to see so far, and to feel ancient ground under her boots.

As winter ended, she worked on her garden. It was pretty and had good soil. There were not too many perennial weeds, apart from couch grass, and even that she found fascinating, as she searched for its pointed root and got it out. The work was satisfying.

The only downside was how steep most of the garden was, and all the sun was at the top, hard to reach without stout boots. The level bit was near the house and in shade a lot of the time. But Hannah was a positive person and she made the best of it. She found a little cast-iron table and chairs in a reclamation yard that she wire-brushed and painted white, so when summer finally came she could at least take a glass of wine outside.

However, on her way to the postbox lay a garden she coveted. Not directly visible from the road, it was tucked away between two houses, both of which had gardens of their own, so this one wasn't part of their property. She looked at it every time she went to post a letter, but couldn't work out to which house it belonged. Little parcels of land belonging to houses not immediately adjacent to them were a feature of this village, she discovered: relics possibly of property once owned but since sold off.

She longed to get her hands on this garden. It was level, a nice square shape, got the sun all day and had some lovely plants. It was also very overgrown and it was this overgrown-ness that made her covet it so much. She didn't want to own it, but she desperately wanted to put it in order. No one seemed to be paying it any attention at all and it seemed a terrible waste. She spotted a wooden gate hiding under a lot of a climbing plant that might well prove to be honey-suckle. You had to go along a snicket to reach it, and its inaccessibility made it even more appealing.

She determined to find out whom it belonged to and ask if she could tend it for them. She'd do it for nothing, just for the pleasure of seeing those borders cleared, the apple tree pruned and the little vegetable patch productive again. It didn't seem to be attached to a house, but she'd got used to that concept.

Ivy at the shop knew everything.

'Oh, now, that belongs to Mrs Gillyflower. She's in hospital at the moment. She used to spend all her time in that garden. It'll break her heart to see it so over-grown when she comes out. If she comes out,' she added gloomily.

What a wonderful name, thought Hannah, ignoring the gloom and instantly seeing Mrs Gillyflower as a trim little woman, brown as a nut, her hair in a bun, with eyes as bright as a bird's, knowing every plant by name and where it came from.

'Would she mind if I looked after it for her? It breaks my heart to see it like that too.'

Ivy considered, not being one to make snap deci-sions. 'Well, I don't see the harm in it. You wouldn't be doing one of those makeovers, would you, like they have on television? Putting down slabs? Painting the fence purple?'

'Certainly not!' Hannah hastened to reassure her. 'I'd just tend the beds that are there, get the veg garden clear of weeds and maybe put some potatoes in? Some beans? So Mrs Gillyflower has something nice to look at when she gets back.'

'Well then, I'm sure that would be fine,' said Ivy, after inspecting Hannah for a while longer.

Hannah walked home and noticed that the house with work going on was developing a rather smart conservatory. She would like a conservatory herself and, when she had worked out where one could go, would save up and have one built. But her mind was really on the garden. It was her secret garden.

Then it began to rain. Day after day, water poured down the gullies and gutters, filled the water butts and made the little stream at the end of the lane flood the road. Mrs Gillyflower's garden became more and more overgrown. Hannah could hardly bear to see the hellebores that had flowered so bravely in the late spring covered up with nettles and goosegrass. The celandines, which had looked so optimistic and cheerful, were now greedily taking over.

Every time Hannah went to the shop she asked after Mrs Gillyflower. Apparently she was getting on well and it was hoped she would be home soon. Hannah was beside herself with frustration at not being able to start work on the garden. The moment the rain stopped, Hannah put her garden tools into her wheelbarrow and, ignoring her own garden, wheeled it down the road and started work.

She staggered home some hours later, exhausted. She had cleared half the vegetable patch and created a new compost heap for the weeds. As she watched the water pour into her bath, sending up wafts of soothing lavender salts, she hoped she wouldn't have to bag up all those weeds and take them to the tip. The council made compost of them, so it was all right, but the work! And Hannah really wanted to make inroads into the flower beds.

It was a few days later before Hannah was able to go

back and she was pleasantly surprised to see how much she'd achieved. She knew she'd worked hard – her muscles were still reminding her – but she didn't remember making a start on that front border or, indeed, finishing the vegetable patch. But as it had definitely been her plan for that day, she carried on from where she'd left off.

There was a second pile of weeds next to the compost heap that she didn't remember leaving there, but it was probably why she'd been thinking about taking some of the garden waste to the tip. She added to the pile and thought how wonderful the garden would be when the roses were out. There was a philadelphus in the corner that would fill the garden with fragrance too.

There were some lovely shrubs in the flower border, but Hannah felt when she'd finished weeding it might look a bit empty, so she made a list of things that were pretty and easy that she would either buy or cadge from neighbours. Old-fashioned aquilegias that Mrs Gillyflower was sure to call 'granny's bonnets', snapdragons, marguerites, pinks and hardy geraniums. She'd put some sweet williams in the veg patch for planting out next year when they would flower and, of course, some of Mrs Gillyflower's namesake – wallflowers.

Every time Hannah went, there seemed to be a bit more done than she remembered doing. Not a huge amount, but just a bit. After a while she stopped thinking about it.

Then, in May, Hannah was really busy, and it was

nearly the end of the month before she was able to go to Mrs Gillyflower's again. She had checked on the old lady's progress and Ivy at the shop was able to tell her she'd be out of hospital soon, so things were getting urgent. Then came the morning when Hannah was woken by birdsong and even before the sun was properly up, before she'd had time for more than a cup of coffee, she was down there, overjoyed to be back again.

It was in surprisingly good order. The front border, nearest to the road, which she had more or less cleared, was still weed-free, although the rest of the countryside seemed to be going mad. The vegetable patch was still clear too. She spent a few minutes being surprised, then settled down to work, determined to make up for lost time.

She was leaning backwards to relieve the strain on her back when she heard a male voice.

'Hello!'

It didn't come from the road, but from behind her. She turned and saw a man actually in the garden.

'What are you doing here?' she demanded, fright making her abrupt.

'Actually, that's my line.'

He was rather attractive and strangely relaxed, considering he'd discovered a trespasser.

Hannah took a nervous step back, into the flower bed. 'Is it?'

'Well, my line, my garden – practically the same thing.'

'It's not your garden. It's Mrs Gillyflower's!' Ivy at

the shop wouldn't have given her the wrong information.

'I'm her nephew and heir.'

'Well, she's not dead, so you can't be her heir, yet!' She paused. 'She's not dead, is she?'

Tears sprang to her eyes at the thought, although she'd never met Mrs Gillyflower. Working in her garden had made her feel she was an old friend, possibly even a favourite aunt. She didn't want her to die, at least, not until she'd seen her garden once more.

'No,' said the man, 'but I'm afraid she won't be able to live on her own again.'

'Oh.'

'She'll have to go into sheltered accommodation. I'm doing up her house so we can rent it out, to help fund her care.'

So the neat little woman with the bird-like eyes and the bun at the back wouldn't walk round the flower beds, admire the veg patch and suggest where the sweet peas should go, happy to see her garden blooming and productive. Hannah sighed. She'd worked terribly hard to that end and now this man was here and had taken her project from her. His being attractive made it worse, not better.

'I'd better go.' She began to gather up her tools, trying not to cry.

'Do you have to? I was really appreciating your help. I've been taken up with the house and haven't been able to do all that much.'

'So you've been gardening here too?'

'Of course! You must have noticed. I thought I'd done quite a lot!' He seemed indignant.

Hannah sighed again. 'I suppose I did notice, I just – chose to ignore it, thought . . . I don't know what I thought.'

'You thought the gardening fairies did it?'

Hannah bit back a sudden smile. It wasn't funny. 'Well, *you* obviously thought they did!' she accused him. 'Otherwise why didn't you stop me? I was trespassing!'

'But in a good way! I was delighted to have help. Between us we're getting on really well! It does seem a shame to stop now.'

'I've worked incredibly hard for nothing!'

'No, you haven't. At least, you were doing it for nothing before.'

'No, I wasn't! I was doing it for Mrs Gillyflower! I imagined her coming back from hospital, dreading to see her garden overgrown and finding it all wonderful.' She paused. 'I feel such a fool.'

'There's no need to feel a fool.'

'I should have noticed the house – which one is it?'

'The one on the corner with the new conservatory. You couldn't possibly have guessed this was its garden. It's going to make it quite difficult to sell if we have to, the garden being so far away.'

'It obviously didn't bother your aunt. It was – is – a lovely garden.'

'Yes, and she *will* see it. She can't come back to live, but she could see the garden and she will appreciate your kindness. As I do. You're a very kind person.'

At that moment Hannah didn't feel kind, she felt stupid, and it wasn't pleasant.

'I won't be able to get it all done on my own,' the man went on. 'It would be wonderful if you could help.'

'And what do I get out of it?' asked Hannah, in an effort to sound tough.

He smiled and shrugged. 'The usual? A really good dinner, cooked by me, fine wine, brandy. Are you single, by the way?'

Hannah tossed her head, sure that he knew she was. 'Are you?'

'Yes.'

'You can't bribe me with offers of food, you know.'

'What can I bribe you with, then?'

Hannah had had time to think about this. 'If I help you get this garden in order for your aunt, I want you to help me get my garden in order.'

'You mean you neglected your garden so you could do this one?'

'Not entirely, but it needs terracing.'

This idea had only just occurred to her, but it was a good one.

'Well, I could do that, I suppose,' he said thoughtfully. 'But couldn't we do the meal thing too? I've been quite lonely since I've been down here. It seems to be mostly young families and retired people.'

'We could go for a drink. The pub's quite good. It does food, too.'

'But I want to try out the new kitchen.' His eyes

crinkled at the corners as he smiled. 'My name's Edward, Edward Gillyflower.'

A most inappropriate thought flickered into Hannah's head as she gave him her name. If she married this man she'd be Mrs Gillyflower and this garden might actually become hers. It was a ridiculous idea and she dismissed it instantly, but she still smiled.

'Well then, Mr Gillyflower, if you promise to terrace my garden, we might well have a deal.'

'It will be my pleasure!' he said. 'Where is your house?'

'Come with me and I'll show you. I didn't have any breakfast. I'll make you a bacon sandwich.'

'If I call you Hannah, will you call me Edward?'

'Maybe.'

At that he hooked his arm through hers and together they walked up the hill to Hannah's house.

The Bench

BY ESTHER FREUD

*S*unday morning and it was quiet in the Maguire kitchen, just the swish of the newspaper, the zap and ping of the DS, the low rumble of the television through the half-closed door. Kate took a long drink of her tea and looked out through the window. The horse chestnut at the end of the garden was always the first to turn – its leaves darkening to copper, the bonnet of its canopy blazing in the autumn sun. Kate glanced over at her husband, unshaven, hair muzzed, eyes fixed to the sports pages of the paper, as they would be for hours.

She'd like to get the children out and force them on a walk, but years of experience had taught her that without an ally she had no chance of tearing them from their screens. 'What?' They'd look at her. 'It's the weekend!' And the thought of her husband's perplexed face as she suggested that they all get some fresh air before lunch stopped her into silence.

'Right,' she said to herself, and she started clearing plates from the table. I suppose I could start chopping vegetables for a soup. But just then her phone burst with the flurry of a text.

Fancy a trip to a pop-up shop in Manningtree? It was Jen.

No idea what that is, Kate texted back. *But pick me up anyway!*

Brett Maguire looked up as his wife ran from the room. Why was she so restless? Always trying to make something happen when what was actually happening was absolutely fine. Had she always been like that? He tipped back his chair and remembered the girl she'd been when they first met. How they used to lie together on the old striped sofa in his flat, listening to music, smiling into each other's eyes. She wasn't rushing round anywhere then, suggesting boat trips and ballroom dancing classes. She'd been content to spend half of Sunday in her dressing gown. It was what he'd loved about her. One of the many things he'd loved.

'You don't mind, do you?' She was back, hair brushed, eyes lit up with mascara. 'I'm going out with Jen. I shouldn't be long. There are sausages in the fridge. Put them in the oven if I'm not back by one.'

There was a hoot from outside and the shadow of Jen's black car blocking the window.

'See you later then.' Brett went back to his paper. Their youngest daughter Ella frowned up from her DS game.

'Mum . . .' but it was too late, she was out of the door.

*

The pop-up shop was on the outskirts of the town, in a furniture maker's warehouse, cleared out for the purpose. Instead of furniture there were textiles, toys, pictures, clothes. Everything handmade and individually priced with stationers' tags tied on with ribbon. There were rush mats spread over the soft grey boards of the floor and pale seascapes framed in driftwood. Jen took a large basket and began to heap in treasure. A tan wool dog with a row of suckling puppies. Five wooden spoons so elegantly turned they deserved to be stroked. Kate held back. She admired a painting of small figures standing at the shore and sat longingly on a chaise longue draped with a red and cream striped throw. But even as she fingered the wool and silken threads, she imagined it scrunched with chocolatey fingers, shredded by the claws of the kitten they'd bought last spring and, anyway, she noticed with relief, it cost several hundred pounds. Instead, she bought a single spoon, the length of her forearm, its grain wound round in seams of amber. In order to resist further temptation, she wandered out into the yard behind the shop. The yard was small, paved with cobbles and hemmed in on three sides with red tiled roofs.

'I'm finding the most fantastic things,' Jen called to her as she struggled past the back door with a reconditioned lamp, and so Kate sat on a bench and closed her eyes. Bright sun streamed down on her, tickling her face, and the boards of the bench cradled her back with its two wide planks.

'Did you find anything you liked?'

There was a creak of wood as someone sat down beside her. A man, low voiced, a trace of Europe in his accent.

'I'm trying to resist,' she told him. 'Although, if this bench was for sale I'd definitely be tempted.'

'It is,' the man said quietly. 'It's one of mine.'

And he told her that once a year he allowed his workshop to be taken over and turned into a shop. It forced him to stop and take a holiday.

Kate opened her eyes and looked at him. Slight, greying, hands ridged and grooved with work.

'So what will you do for the rest of the week?' she asked.

'Paris,' he told her, and he described for her the paintings he'd see there, the food he'd eat, the friends he'd meet up with, the walks he'd take along the River Seine.

Kate let her eyes sink shut and imagine herself there too. A café table. A carafe of wine, a meal of *moules-frites*. She tried not to think of her family, slumped at home with the heating on, the mess of the kitchen table, a duvet dragged across the sitting-room floor.

The man was telling her about his childhood. The island in Finland where he'd spent his summers. How he and his brothers would take a boat and drift out on to the flat midsummer sea, lit up by the sun that never set. At midnight, fireworks would shoot up from every neighbouring island, and they'd row as fast as they could to try and catch the sparks. But several years ago his mother died, leaving no will, and the house that had belonged to them all, the wooden house with its metal stove, and its sauna from where they'd run and throw themselves into the water, was in danger of being lost as he and his brothers failed to agree.

'I'm so sorry,' Kate shook her head and she told him about her own family. How her mother favoured the youngest of her sisters, setting her up in a catering business, paying the deposit on a flat. The bitterness of it, the unfairness, even now forced tears into her eyes. 'It's split our family apart.'

She hadn't known until that moment that it had, and she could feel the man's sympathy, the quiet way he listened. Very gently he talked about his own children who lived with his ex-wife, and how much he hoped they'd find their way, how much he hoped they'd always get along. Kate told him about her eldest girl and the ferocious arguments that flared between them.

'No one in my life has ever made me so angry,' she confessed, and she described her blonde-haired, fair-skinned daughter and the barbs that flew from her rosebud mouth. They laughed together then, her eyes still closed, her heart as light as a balloon.

'So,' she felt him turn towards her. 'What will you be cooking with your wooden spoon?'

'I'll hang it on the wall,' she said. 'And go out to the pub.'

And she laughed again, and told him what she'd order in the pub, and when she finished he insisted they have pudding. Hot chocolate soufflé, plum crumble, ice cream. After strong, black coffee they decided they'd surely need a walk and, for twenty minutes at least, they compared the pleasures of trudging through the mulch of wood and bracken on the disused railway, to the satisfying crunch of pebbles marching the length of the estuary at low tide.

Back in the yard, the sun was arcing down into the afternoon, slanting in over the roofs, bathing them in warmth, and as they talked and walked, their stomachs full, there was nothing but the two of them in the whole small town.

'Kate!'

Jen was calling to her, the shadow of her laden form forcing open her eyes. 'I've brought the car round. I was hooting for you.' She sounded aggrieved, and as Kate stood up, the man slipped away round the side of the building before she'd had a chance to say goodbye.

'Get anything?' Jen asked, and Kate looked at the bench and saw it had a price tag knotted to its side.

'Yes,' she decided, and as she wrote out her cheque she wondered if it would be the man himself who would deliver it.

There was no one in the house when the bench arrived. Brett couldn't imagine for a minute what it was, when the two burly women lifted it out of the truck. But then he remembered Kate's defiant expression the Sunday before when she said she'd bought a present – for herself.

'Where would you like it?' the first flushed woman

asked and, refusing all offers of help, they heaved it to a spot at the back of the garden, under the horse chestnut tree, against the wide gnarled trunk.

'Yes,' he agreed, 'That's perfect,' even though he knew it was impossible to get a signal here. And he sat down, his computer blinking, forgotten in the house, while the two women walked away. He could feel the tilt of the slats as they held his back, the soft wood of the seat as soothing as a cushion. And he waited, listening to the birds, breathing in the dense smell of the earth.

Kate's heart leapt with fear as she came round the side of the house and saw him waiting for her, his face in shadow, acting, as she'd hoped he would, on the invitation of her address. The forms of her children flashed before her, so confident in the order of their lives, and the solid warmth of her husband's back as she reached out and slid her fingers round him in the night.

'Kate.'

Had she even told him her name? And the thought occurred to her that she could run. She could turn and slam out through the gate and keep running till she reached the main road. But as she moved towards the tree, a leaf swooped down and landed in her hands.

'That's a sign, surely?' she told herself, and she stepped under the canopy of branches and saw that it was Brett.

'Come here.' He put his hand out. 'And talk to me.'

And remembering the luck they'd used to feel in having found each other, he lay down with her along the striped slats of the bench and held her close against him so that even if she'd wanted to, she couldn't get away.

The Whole Truth and Nothing But the Truth

BY TESS GERRITSEN

*Y*ou can't go wrong by telling the truth. That's been drilled into my head since I was a child, but I'm debating the wisdom of that advice as two Los Angeles homicide detectives step into my apartment.

Detective Marcus has grey hair and a gaze like blue icicles. His female partner, Detective Suarez, is a wide-hipped woman with acne scars. Neither one smiles at me, which is what I'd expect, considering the reason for their visit. The news is all over the TV this morning: singer Isabel Lyon, thirty-four, was shot to death last night in her Beverly Hills home. No arrests have been made.

I, Laura McCarthy, am a suspect.

The detectives sit down on my frayed sofa and eye the thrift store lamps. The smell of burned toast hangs in the air and the roar of a passing city bus rattles the window.

When Richard and I married five years ago, this apartment was what we could afford. Now that I'm divorced and supporting myself on a receptionist's salary, it's even more of a struggle to keep up with the rent. It's a universe away from Isabel's world, where furniture comes from Italy, not the resale shop. Marcus and Suarez need only take a glance around to see that I have every reason to be bitter.

'How well did you know Isabel Lyon?' Detective Marcus asks.

'Not very well. I'd heard of her, of course, through my husband Richard.'

'You mean your ex-husband.'

It's a callous remark and I look away. 'Thank you for reminding me,' I say softly.

'Did you and Isabel ever meet?'

'Only once. It was a year ago, at her release party. My husband – my *ex*-husband – played keyboard for her last album. All the band members and their wives were invited to her house. I'd never been to Beverly Hills. I grew up in Fresno and I'd never even met a celebrity before. I had no idea what to wear . . .'

My voice drifts off. I think about that night, when I'd stood on the ballroom balcony, staring down at her garden. There, among the marble statues and fountains, Isabel and Richard were kissing. I remember how the wind wrapped the hem of her flowing silk gown around his legs, as though to enfold him in her web. And I remember how she glanced up at me, not with any look of guilt that she'd been caught embracing my husband. No, she acted as if I were invisible. Something to be ignored.

'That was a year ago?' asks Marcus.

'Yes.'

'What happened then?'

I shake my head and sigh. 'It's such an old story, isn't it? You think you're happily married, and along comes someone new and prettier and a whole lot richer. Our divorce was final four months ago. A week later, he married Isabel. They went to Capri for their honeymoon.'

I look around at my apartment, at the knick-knacks that Richard and I had so lovingly acquired during our marriage. Such sad little things, I realise now, cheap souvenirs that only struggling newly-weds would covet.

'I've never been to Capri,' I add, unnecessarily.

'And your feelings about Isabel?'

They are both watching me, waiting to see if I'm a liar or a truth-teller. *You can't go wrong by telling the truth.*

'She stole my husband.' I stare straight at Marcus. 'I wish I could have pulled that trigger myself.'

There is the truth, and then there is *the truth*, unfiltered and straight from the gut. They know which version they've just heard and I spy the twitch of a smile on Suarez's lips. Like me, she is not beautiful and we recognise in each other the shared experience of the discarded woman. We are not like the lucky, leggy Isabels of the world.

Marcus asks: 'Where were you last night, Ms McCarthy?'

'Here. I was home all night.'

'Can anyone verify that?'

'Ask my neighbour, Carla Willis. She's in apartment four, next door. She called me last night, on my land-line, and we spoke.'

'What time did she call?'

'Around ten.' I pause. 'The TV said Isabel was killed around nine. It's a three-hour drive from here, so there's no way I could have done it. If that's what you're thinking.'

'We'll need to confirm that call with your neigh-bour,' he says automatically, but I can already see he's mentally checked me off his suspect list.

No, I couldn't have done it, but I know who the obvious suspect is.

'Did Richard kill her?' I ask.

Marcus raises an eyebrow at my blunt question. 'Why do you think he would?'

'Because he found out what kind of person he mar-ried.'

'And what would that be?'

'A woman who's used to getting everything she wants. A woman who has it all and still isn't satisfied. So she steals the one precious thing I have.'

I look out the window at the dry-cleaning business across the street and brush my hand across my eyes.

'Now he has more money than he'll ever need. And all I wanted was a husband who'd love me.'

'Yet you still love him.' For the first time, it's Suarez speaking. Her voice is softer, gentler than I'd im-agined. I look at her and see sympathy in her eyes.

'Yes,' I admit. 'It's not easy to forget five years of

marriage. I can't just slice off a piece of my heart. I believed in him. I believed in his talent. I thought, as long as we had each other, nothing else mattered.' I look around at my apartment, at the second-hand furniture. 'We were going to make it out of here some day. That's what I believed. We'd have children and money and we'd be in love for ever.'

'But Isabel changed all that,' says Suarez.

'Yes.'

'And you must be really, truly pissed at him.'

I don't answer her; I don't need to. She's supplied her own answer, the one she believes every woman would feel in my position.

'Ms McCarthy, have you seen Richard lately?' asks Marcus.

'Why would I? They live three hours away.'

'Richard claims that last night, at the time his wife was shot to death, he was here in San Diego. With you.'

I stare at him. A moment passes. Through the thin walls, I hear the sound of my neighbour's TV blaring. Carla's TV is always blaring.

'So I'm to be his alibi?' I ask softly.

I turn to Suarez, whose face looks more and more like a friend's.

'It all depends on me, doesn't it? If I tell you he was here with me, it means he's innocent. That he couldn't have done it. But if I tell you he wasn't, then you'll know he lied to you. Which means he must be guilty.' I smile at the irony. 'It's a strange thing, holding his future in my hands. A powerful feeling.'

'*Was* he here?' asks Marcus.

Through the thin wall, I hear Carla's phone ringing, but I stay focused on Suarez. I can see she understands how delicious the temptation must be for me, and why I'm taking so long answering. I'm savouring the moment, thinking about Isabel's party, when I'd stood on her balcony. That night, I'd looked down at her and thought: you have everything and I have so little. How unfair it is, that one selfish woman like you should have all this, yet still want more.

'Just tell us Richard wasn't here last night,' says Suarez, 'and we'll take it from there.'

Oh yes, she wants Richard to pay, not just for murder but also for what he did to me. For what too many men do to wives with whom they've grown bored.

You can't go wrong telling the truth.

'Richard wasn't here,' I answer. 'I was home alone. All night.'

They exchange satisfied looks of *We've got him*.

There's a knock on my door.

It's my neighbour Carla, and even though I explain to her that I have visitors, she blurts out: 'Richard just called me. I can't believe he had the nerve. He wants to know if you've unplugged your phone, because you aren't picking up.'

'Can we talk about this later?' I quickly cut in.

'I never saw that side of him, not once in all these

years. Oh Laura, you poor thing. I can't believe what he said to you last night.'

'Excuse me,' interrupts Marcus. 'Are you the neighbour in apartment four?'

Carla frowns at him. 'Yes. Why?'

'I'm Detective Marcus, Los Angeles PD. Were you talking about Ms McCarthy's ex-husband?'

'Yeah, the bastard. He was here, yelling at her. Things you can't imagine.'

'When?'

'Last night. You can hear everything through these thin walls. He was screaming, calling her a—'

Carla stops, unwilling to repeat the profanity that Richard shouted. The words that all my neighbours probably heard.

'I was worried about Laura, so I called to find out if she needed any help.'

'I was fine, Carla. I told you I could handle him.'

'Well, I think you should have called the police.'

'Are you certain it was her ex-husband in here last night?' says Marcus.

'I should know his voice. I've lived next door to them for years.'

'And what time did you hear them arguing?'

'It was around ten. Interrupted my favourite TV show.'

'Are you willing to sign a statement to that effect, Ms Willis?' Suarez asks.

'Of course,' says Carla. 'Because it's the truth.'

And I, clearly, am the liar. The bitter ex-wife who's so hungry for revenge that her word can't be trusted.

I sit stony-faced with shame as the two detectives leave my apartment. I ignore my phone, which rings, again and again. On Caller ID, I recognise a steady succession of familiar numbers, calls from friends and family who are no doubt anxious to gossip about Isabel's murder.

The one person who does not call me is Richard. I don't expect him to. It's far too soon.

I go to my bedroom and remove from its hiding place the CD that Richard recorded a week ago in his music studio. It's a half-hour's worth of him shouting hurtful, disgusting words, words that had boomed from my stereo system last night at ten, when I knew Carla would hear them.

Nothing I said to the police was a lie. Every question they asked, I answered with the truth. Last night, I *was* home alone. And Richard was with Isabel, doing exactly what he said he would do.

I take the CD into the bathroom, smash it into tiny pieces with a hammer and flush the fragments down the toilet.

At six, I change into my best dress and put on bright lipstick. I drive to a restaurant where I have always wanted to dine, but could never afford. There I sip a glass of champagne, thinking about the last time I tasted such a treat.

It was the night of Isabel's party, when I stood on her balcony, looking down at the garden. I remember gazing across the statues and fountains and thinking how lovely it would be to some day own such a place with Richard. How lovely for us to never again worry about money. To see Capri.

I watched my husband and Isabel embrace, her green dress a swirl of silk. I remember her disdainful glance when she noticed that I was staring at them from above. I watched them walk away arm in arm, Isabel with her newly claimed prize. She never looked back, but simply strolled onward into the shadows with my husband.

She didn't see that I was smiling.

This champagne does taste lovely. I think I could get used to it.

The Coiled Serpent

BY DAISY GOODWIN

*M*r Palmer was working on the thirty pieces of silver when the bell rang. He had developed a shade of mauve that gave the blood money just the right tinge. It was his palette that made him the discerning customer's choice, that and the ambition of his designs, which paid for these premises in Bond Street. He hoped that in time his art would be sufficiently recognised that he might one day be able to display a royal warrant. He was as entitled to one as the jewellers next door, having worked on the Prince of Wales as well as his sons, the Duke of York and the late Duke of Clarence.

He heard Betty's voice.

'There's someone here to see you, Mr Palmer, a lady.'

Palmer put down his needle. 'We'll finish this later, Sam. Another hour and it will be done.'

Sam got up from the table where he had been lying face down and stretched his broad shoulders. Christ and his disciples were ranged across his back, starting with St Thomas on the right through to Judas on the left. Jesus was blessing the bread and wine somewhere to the left of Sam's spine.

It was Palmer's most magnificent piece yet. He was going to display it at the Paris Exhibition, along with his rendition of M. Eiffel's wonderful tower, which ran up the back of Sam's calf.

Palmer pushed back the heavy velvet *portière* that hung over the door to his studio and went into the small waiting room. He saw that Betty had been correct in describing his visitor as a 'lady'. She was wearing a navy-blue costume trimmed with fur and a neat round hat with a veil. She was so impeccably turned out that Palmer wondered if she might be foreign. English ladies tended to look comfortable in their clothes rather than elegant.

Instinctively, Palmer looked for a patch of skin and he saw a thin band of flesh between her glove and the top of her sleeve. He could see from the dusting of fair hairs that she was a blonde, with waxy white skin that would be the perfect background for one of his more delicate designs. Too often the detail was obscured by darker hair.

He introduced himself and said, 'How can I help you, madam?'

He did not pause for her to give her name. His female clients, the respectable ones at least, preferred to remain anonymous. The woman lifted her veil, and he could see that she was young, in her early twenties, he guessed. Her eyes were a very pale blue.

108

'I was given your name by Lady Tav— by a friend of mine.'

She stopped, blushing at her own slip. Palmer could hear from her voice that she was American and, from the size of the diamonds hanging from her earlobes, clearly a rich one: perhaps she was one of the famous 'dollar princesses' who had traded their fortune for a titled husband. But as the flush spread across her cheeks, Palmer thought she was pretty enough to attract any man, heiress or not.

'My friend said that you were the best in London . . . for what I have in mind.'

Palmer nodded, acknowledging the truth of this.

She began to peel off her kid glove, revealing long, tapering fingers.

Palmer said, 'I have some pattern books I can show you. They include some very fine Japanese motifs that are very popular with my lady clients.'

'Actually, I know what I want.'

She had her glove off now and held up a white wrist, crossed by thin blue veins. She pointed to a spot an inch below her palm.

'I want a snake that goes around my wrist like this,' she traced the route with her finger, 'and ends up with its tail in its mouth. In green, the colour of jade.' She looked at him, her outstretched hand trembling slightly. 'I hope it won't be too painful.'

Palmer looked into her limpid blue eyes and said slowly, 'I am afraid that the wrist is one of the more sensitive areas of the body. If you are worried about the pain, may I suggest a . . . a fleshier place.'

'No, it has to be the wrist. That's where my friend has hers – she covers it with a diamond bracelet.'

She smiled and Palmer felt his middle-aged heart flutter. It was a long time since he had been so close to such a lovely young woman. And her skin really was like alabaster. He imagined tracing a butterfly over one white shoulder. The woman was still speaking with her American twang. Palmer thought she was enjoying the sound of her own voice, almost as if she had not used it much lately.

'I wondered why Lady Tavistock, I mean my friend, always wore the bracelet, but I didn't dare ask her. English women can be very funny about direct questions.'

She frowned.

'But then one day I saw her washing her hands – she had taken the bracelet off and I saw the snake. Lady Tavistock saw me staring and she said it was quite the fashion now to have them done, and she told me your name. I was surprised, really, that she was so nice about it. She's a very old friend of my husband's and I think she was surprised that he had married an American girl. Though not as much as I am to be married to a viscount. Why, before I came over here, I thought you said vis-cont.'

She giggled and her hand flew to cover her mouth. Palmer noticed that her engagement ring sported a decidedly lesser diamond to the ones in her ears.

Clearly, she had brought more than beauty to the marriage.

'Well, then I knew I had to have one. I may come from Cincinnati, but I know how to be fashionable.'

She reached into her reticule and took out a Morocco leather case. Inside was a bracelet dense with diamonds.

'I thought if I brought this with me, you could make sure that the tattoo fits under it exactly. We are going to stay at Warwick Castle next week and the Prince of Wales will be there. I want to be quite the thing when I meet him. I hear he likes fashionable women.'

Palmer looked at the gems glittering against the blue velvet lining of the case and at his visitor's white fingers. He found himself trying to swallow the lump of anxiety that was forming in his throat. He wondered if this girl could really be unaware of what she was asking him to do. But possibly he was misjudging her; perhaps she knew very well.

He thought of the three other wrists he had adorned with green snakes at thirty guineas a time. Wrists that belonged to some of the most experienced women in London. He found it hard to believe that this radiant young woman was part of that particular club. He found himself shaking his head almost without realising it.

'Excuse me for asking this, but does your husband know that you are here?'

She looked at him in astonishment. 'No, of course not. That would spoil the surprise. He thinks that I don't understand anything, you see. He calls me his little savage, as if I'd grown up with feathers in my hair instead of in the biggest home in Cincinnati.' She shook her head and the diamonds sparkled.

Palmer looked at her slender white wrist with longing. It would be a rare pleasure, he thought, to add the finishing touch to such perfection. Really, he would almost pay to be able to work on such a canvas.

'I am sorry, your ladyship, but I don't have the time at the moment for a job of this sort. I am very busy at the moment, finishing off a major piece for the Paris Exhibition.'

This much, at least, was true.

The American blinked. 'But Lady Tavistock told me it wouldn't take more than an hour. Surely, you could manage that. And, of course, I will pay you whatever you ask – I have my own money, you see. My father thought his girl should be independent.'

She put her head on one side and half lowered her lashes. Palmer guessed that her father had denied her nothing.

He caught a whiff of her scent as she tilted her head and he felt his resolve weaken, but then he thought of the three other snake tattoos.

'It's not a question of money. A tattoo is irrevocable. For some people, they bring back pleasant memories, but for others they can be a permanent reminder of a mistake.'

She frowned. 'But I'm not making a mistake.'

'With respect, your ladyship, I don't think you have all the information.'

She stared at him, then dropped her chin sharply and stood up.

'Well, I shall just have to go elsewhere.'

He shook his head. 'I am afraid you won't find anyone else who can do that design. That particular shade of green is my own invention.'

The American was trying to pull on her gloves, but her hands were shaking so much that she tore the delicate kid leather with her nail.

'I suppose it's because I'm American that you won't do it. Sometimes I wish I had never come to this horrible, unfriendly country.'

Mr Palmer saw tears in her eyes. He opened the door for her. 'Goodbye, your ladyship.'

She swept past without looking at him. He could see one tear had escaped and was rolling down her cheek.

A month later, Palmer was working on the tricky twist at the corner of the Mona Lisa's mouth when he heard the bell. This time, she was dressed in a pink-and-white striped silk with a matching parasol. As he walked into the room, she looked up and smiled at him warmly.

'Oh Mr Palmer, I don't know how to thank you. I was so angry with you that day and now I could kiss you. When I think what could have happened.'

She squeezed his hand fervently.

'When you refused to give me the tattoo, I thought I would wear the bracelet the first night at Warwick

Castle anyway. But when I came down to dinner, I saw that people were looking at me. I mean, they are always looking at me, but they were looking at the bracelet. I thought that they were admiring it, but when my husband saw it, I realised my mistake. He told me to take it off. He was looking at my wrist as if it was on fire or something, and then when he saw that there was nothing there, he picked it up and kissed me – here.'

She pointed to the place on her wrist where two blue veins crossed.

'He didn't want to tell me what he had been looking for, but I can be very persuasive.' She smiled. 'He told me what the tattoo meant.' She coloured. 'Why, I have met the Prince of Wales now, and he's old enough to be my father. That's not a club I want to join and, besides, I love my husband.'

She placed her white hand on Palmer's arm.

'I would have lost him if you had put the snake on my wrist. I was so angry with you then, but I reckon now that you saved me. Am I right?'

Palmer nodded. 'As I said, I knew that your ladyship did not have all the information.'

She opened wide her pale blue eyes. 'You did me a kindness, Mr Palmer, and I would like to repay you. A hundred guineas seems the least I can do.'

Palmer closed his eyes for a moment. 'I don't want money.' He took a deep breath. 'But there is one thing I would ask in return.'

He gazed at her luminous face.

'The chance to practise my art.'

And he swayed slightly as he thought of the butterfly he would put on the smooth white skin of her shoulder.

The Safety Net

BY SOPHIE HANNAH

*H*ere he is at last – the man I've been waiting for. Physically, he is exactly right: about six feet tall, short dark hair, broad-shouldered and heavy without being fat, no facial hair. He is perfect in every detail.

If that sounds romantic, it's not meant to. There's nothing romantic about my state of mind at the moment, as I sit here gripping my glass of red wine, crying, staring at the television screen.

I've been waiting for this man for four and a half years. This particular man, not just one of any number of men. Of course, there was a time when he was not 'this particular man', though he had the potential to become him. The transformation took place on 22 January 2011. At half past midnight.

I haven't known his name for the past four and a half years, and I still don't. All I knew was that he needed to be of the physical type I have described. His personality didn't matter, as long as it was the kind that might commit a violent crime. Murder, ideally.

No, sorry, that's wrong. The man I needed wasn't someone who was merely capable of killing; I was waiting for an actual murderer, someone who had killed already.

His choice of victim mattered too. If, for example, he was a drug-fuelled waster who had killed another drug-fuelled waster in a street fight, that wouldn't have been any good for my purposes. That killer would not have been the one I was waiting for. No, I needed someone whose victim had been harmless and innocent – female, too, ideally, so that the crime was as abhorrent as a murder could be. I was waiting for an evil man who had killed a helpless woman – perhaps someone so evil that he was beyond hope of redemption.

Over the years, this idea has terrified me so much that, many times, I have considered abandoning my plan. A voice inside me kept screaming, 'I don't want anything to do with that sort of person.' Time and time again, I had to remind myself that I wouldn't need to have anything to do with him, once I found him. There would be no contact whatsoever between us; I wouldn't even find out his name, if I was lucky.

If I'm lucky, I will feel better once I've done this. That's all I want: to feel better. I don't know if it's possible, but I have to try.

My final requirement was that the murder had to have been committed in or near Nottingham. So many specifics that needed to be in alignment – to be honest, I'm surprised I've had to wait only four and a half years; I expected it to be more like ten.

Anyway, I've found him now, which is all that matters. He's where I always knew he would be: on the television news. I stare at the police artist's sketch of him, and listen as Rosemary Vickers, a detective superintendent with Nottinghamshire Police, describes what he did: on 22 January, at half past midnight, he attacked and killed eighteen-year-old Nadine Mc-Gahan in a park in Nottingham. I try not to listen too closely to the details of what he did to her; I would have nightmares if I allowed myself to think about it.

I think instead about my ex, Owen, who dumped me five years ago, making sure to tell me everything he'd found unattractive and unappealing about me during our two-year relationship. I haven't been able to like myself since, even though most of the things he said were lies. My friends think it's crazy: if I know he was talking rubbish, why let it get to me?

I never explain to anybody – it's too humiliating – but there is a perfectly rational explanation: true or not, the fact that the person closer to me than anyone in the world wanted to hurt me enough to say all those things has to mean something about me, something I'd rather not put into words, even to myself.

Shortly after our break-up, Owen moved to Nottingham. He is not quite six feet tall, not as broad-shouldered as the man the police artist has drawn, and the nose is different, but there's enough of a resemblance. I pick up the phone and dial the number that Rosemary Vickers is urging me and millions of other viewers to dial if we know anything.

*

Things have moved quickly – or maybe it seems so only to me, after my years-long wait. There's a female detective in my living room.

'Tell me everything you know about Owen Trinder,' she says.

I tell her he's a primary-school teacher, that in his spare time he does something called 'geo-cacheing', which he described to me many times but I never entirely understood. He's forty-three, originally from Doncaster.

She asks some questions I wasn't expecting: what alcoholic drinks did he drink when I knew him? Did he smoke? Was our sex life normal? Was he ever violent towards me?

I don't bother to ask whether breaking my heart in a particularly hurtful way counts as violence; I say no.

And finally, the big question: how certain am I that the man in the police artist's sketch is Owen?

'It's him,' I say.

I planned to extend my lie and say that when I knew Owen, he often wore a black-and-orange zip-up coat exactly like the one the man in the police artist's sketch is wearing, but I decide against it. That's something that could be proved to be untrue. Owen didn't wear a coat like that, ever, and people who knew him when I did might come forward to say so. Whereas no one can prove that my belief that one man's face resembles another's is a lie; it often happens that one person spots a resemblance that another can't see even once it's been pointed out. I will always be able to pretend, convincingly, that I looked at the face in the sketch and saw Owen's features.

'You're sure it's Owen Trinder?' the detective asks.

'There's no doubt in my mind,' I say.

She nods. 'Very interesting,' she says, with a small smile.

Oh, God, oh, no. What have I done?

It is two days since the detective's visit and I am in hell. She said she'd keep me informed, but I haven't heard from her, and she isn't returning my calls. What did her smile mean? Did she know I was lying? How could she possibly?

Am I being punished for what I've done? When I planned it, it didn't seem so bad: follow the news, follow *Crimewatch*, wait for a man in Nottingham who looks superficially like Owen to commit a brutal crime, then tell the police I think Owen might have done it, based on the photofit I saw on TV. They would question him; he would produce his alibi and a DNA sample, and be off the hook, with no permanent harm done.

I wanted to give him a shock, that's all – I wanted him to suffer in proportion to the suffering he'd caused me. I decided that to be suspected, briefly, of having committed a horrific crime – to fear, however fleetingly, that, in spite of your innocence, you might be charged, tried, found guilty, imprisoned, hated by everyone in the country – would cause approximately the same amount of distress as being dumped in the precise way that I was by Owen. Less, even, because it would be over much sooner.

And I had a safety net in place: if for some reason the police took too long to eliminate Owen from their enquiries, I would confess to my lie. I wouldn't let him suffer that level of fear for more than a few days, a week maximum. What's one week compared with five years of feeling worthless?

I've come up against a problem I didn't anticipate, however: the police aren't keeping me updated. I realise it was naive of me to assume they would. Thank you so much for your help, Miss Elstow – yes, of course we'll make sure you're fully briefed at every stage as our investigation progresses.

How will I know whether I need to confess if they don't tell me what's going on?

And why did the detective smile in that funny way? Why did she say, 'Very interesting'?

I've done something terrible. If I could undo it, I would, but I can't.

The doorbell rings. I leap up, assuming it's the detective who interviewed me, but it isn't. It's Owen.

I have dreamed about this happening, except that in my dreams he isn't angry, as he is now in real life. My dream Owen says he's sorry – he still loves me, was a fool to think he could live without me.

Angry real Owen says, 'It was you, wasn't it? You twisted, evil—'

'I'm sorry,' I say, and I burst into tears.

'Lucky for me, I had two friends who told the police I was with them in a club at the relevant time.'

'I'm so sorry, Owen. I don't know what came over me, I just—'

'You thought I was capable of doing that? To a woman?'

He sees the expression on my face, listens to my silence. That's when the truth hits him; I watch it land, like a physical blow. And I hate myself even more, because, even as I'm apologising, I'm still lying. How can I say, 'I don't know what came over me?' as if it was a sudden impulse, when I've been planning this for years?

'I see.' Owen nods, seeming calmer now. 'You knew it wasn't me, but you rang the police and said it was.'

I just wanted our story to end in a better way, in a way that my pride could live with: he broke her heart, left her in pieces, but she had the last laugh. She decided the whole sewing-prawns-into-curtain-linings thing was so five minutes ago, and went one better: she manipulated the police into suspecting him of murder. I actually imagined people saying this to one another, awestruck admiration in their voices. I guess when you spend as much time on your own as I have over the past few years, your fantasy world starts to seem more real than reality.

I have to try to make it up to him.

'I don't hate you, Owen,' I say shakily. 'I swear I don't. Sometimes, when people hurt each other – like when you said all those vicious things when you left –

it's because of hate, but sometimes it's love, love in pain that lashes out and—'

'You know the funny thing?' Owen talks over me. 'You weren't the only one.'

His words stop me in my tracks. 'What do you mean?'

'Another woman rang the police and said the guy in the sketch was me – even though so many details were wrong: he was too thickset, his nose was bigger. Personally, I didn't see the resemblance.'

'But . . . why?'

Why would anyone do that, unless they were me?

Owen smiles. 'I know what you're thinking: did I dump her too, and did she have the same idea as you? Unlikely.'

'Then what—?'

'Like I said, I was lucky: my two best mates were willing to tell the police I was with them when Nadine McGahan was murdered.'

I breathe in sharply. And then I find I can't breathe, in or out. He didn't say 'willing to', not the first time. Why would he say 'willing to', unless . . . ?

He lifts his sweater, starts to pull his belt out from the loops of his trousers.

'I reckon I've got about another day, while they process my DNA sample.'

As he walks towards me, I can't look away from his eyes: two bottomless chips of ice in his contorted face.

'How long do you reckon you've got?' he says.

Sweet Peas

BY RACHEL HEATH

*I*t may surprise you to know – it certainly did me – that working in a florist's invites questions about happiness. Folk coming in to buy or order flowers are often stilled in front of the variety and choice. They might ask: which flowers make me happiest, which do I think most suitable for giving thanks, which are my favourite or which would be best for an apology or, of course, as a sign of love?

In a florist's, you see people celebrate the high days with wild extravagant bunches and, on the low days, attempt to alleviate sorrow or look for consolation in the right arrangements. Then there are the in-between days to be negotiated too. It's a thought-provoking business.

And so, while I suggest flowers, or bunch the stems, or wrap their chosen display in turquoise paper and Cellophane, they ask which flowers make me happiest, and I say, 'Sweet peas, because of a friend I made last summer.'

Last summer, I was pretty much stymied and heart-broken. I was reluctantly working for a temporary employment agency, which, one week, sent me to a company that was moving offices. They needed someone – me – to sit all alone in their old, abandoned office building and answer the telephone while the new premises were prepared and the telephone lines installed. It sounded like a job that would suit my condition very well.

The offices were on the ground floor of a Victorian terraced house. When I arrived on Monday morning, the front door was already unlocked and the inside door to the offices pushed open to my touch. I walked silently around the empty rooms. In the front room, sunlight fell through the sash window, leaving bleached rectangles on the dusty carpet. A telephone switchboard had been set up on the side of a packing case; beside it was a small wooden chair. Walking through to the next room, I found ceilings that were high and ornate, rooms painted a pale grey, and a dark-blue carpet dented with the marks of recently removed desks and chairs. That was it. Everything was quiet, empty and still.

It was stuffily silent, so I unlocked and opened the window at the front and looked out, blinking at the bright light that bounced off the heat-drenched pavements. I could hear the tinny sound of the summer's hit song being played out of an open window further up the street. When I leaned out and looked up to the right, I could see the green fringes of a park – the feathery tops of the trees and their slender trunks – but there were no people on the pavements and no cars on the street.

These offices are just like the city, I thought, turning round to survey them, and just like me. We're all paused, as though suspended in the heat – empty, weightless and slowed. All was not as it once had been or would shortly become again.

I went to the kitchen to look for a kettle and some coffee, but found only a dry, wilting brown plant sitting next to the sink. I picked off the dead leaves, watered it and carried the plant through to sit on the front windowsill in the sunshine.

The telephone rang and I rushed to answer it.

'A.C. Enterprises. How may I help you?'

'I need to speak to Mr Holmes,' a woman said quickly, sounding breathless. 'It's urgent.'

'I'm sorry, he's not here,' I told her. 'The firm are moving offices, they'll open again in one week. May I take a message?'

There was a silence. I could hear the woman's breath catch as she exhaled. She was thinking it through.

'Gordon Holmes,' she repeated anxiously. 'I need to speak to him.'

'Leave your number and I'll make sure he gets your message.'

'I'm here for the whole summer,' she said. 'Tell him that.'

She left her number and insisted again that it was urgent, and I promised to pass this on.

The day passed quickly. At five o'clock, I closed the

window and phoned the number for the answerphone on which I was supposed to leave any messages. It was then I realised she hadn't left her name.

'A lady rang,' I said into the machine. 'She needs to speak urgently to Mr Holmes. Here's her number.'

I walked home through the empty streets, stopping off at the corner shop to buy my meal for one. I ate it quickly, standing up by the window in my flat, staring at the darkening red sky and drinking glass after glass of tap water. I found myself idly wondering about the mysterious woman and hoping that Mr Holmes had got in touch with her.

The next day, she called again. She sounded calmer this time, more relaxed.

'Did you speak to him? What did he say?'

'I left your number on the message service. That's how it works.'

'I see.' She breathed in. 'Do you know Gordon?'

'I've never met anyone who works here,' I said, enjoying the sound of my voice in the desolate room. A breeze snuck in from the open window and circled my waist, as though inviting me to dance. 'I'm just a temp. Everyone else must be on holiday or at the new offices.'

'Well, I know that feeling.' She laughed. 'Do you mind being on your own?'

'It is a bit odd.' I looked up at the peeling paint hanging off the centre ceiling rose. 'It's certainly quiet.'

'I'm sorry to keep ringing, but would you mind

leaving another message?' She sounded apologetic and a bit ashamed. 'I shouldn't be doing this.'

'I don't mind you ringing at all,' I told her warmly, and meaning it. 'What's your name?'

'It's Annie,' she said. 'Just Annie.'

Annie didn't ring the next day. There was one call about paper supply and another from a man who complained in great detail about something I didn't understand, and who refused to believe that I was the only person in the building. In the end, I held the receiver up in the air for a minute and said, 'See? It's totally quiet, isn't it? There's no one here.'

'Yes,' he said, astonished. 'They really have moved on then?'

On Thursday, when I arrived, I was startled to see a tall man with dark curly hair pacing about the empty rooms. He looked annoyed and uncomfortable, and was fighting to loosen his tie.

'I'm Gordon Holmes,' he blurted out. 'When she calls again, can you tell her to stop? I don't want to speak to her. Tell her that.'

I started to tell him that I didn't think it was any of my business, but he flapped his hand at me and left, very quickly, banging the door behind him. I rushed over to the window and saw him walking fast across the street, still yanking at his tie.

I felt light-headed with worry all day, and when Annie finally called, I wasn't sure how to break the news to her.

'I'm really sorry,' I said awkwardly. 'Mr Holmes came here. He asked you to stop calling.'

'How stupid.' I was relieved to hear a light bubble of laughter in her voice. 'I don't even like him that much. He just stopped calling – don't you hate it when they do that? No explanation, nothing. It drives me mad, it's just so . . . rude.'

'He was quite rude here too. Came and went pretty quickly.'

I wanted her to know I absolutely sympathised with how she felt, that I wasn't play-acting or pretending politeness. I leaned heavily on the edge of the packing case.

'Is he your boyfriend?' I asked.

'Sort of.' I could feel her smile down the phone. 'In truth, it wasn't serious, and I'm too old to be chasing him, demanding answers.'

'He probably won't even have a reason for not calling, not a good one. And that will annoy you even more.'

'You're so right,' she said, sounding relieved. 'That's true.'

And then, because there seemed no reason not to, we carried on chatting. I sat down, leaned back in the wooden chair, and told her about my own broken heart; how my ex-partner had taken me out to dinner and told me that he thought I was reckless and taking too many risks, and that he couldn't support me.

'Why did he say that?'

'I want to open a florist's,' I told her. 'I've been

working towards this for years. It's not some flight of fancy. I've done courses, got experience, written a business plan. I've found a brilliant location and had a start-up loan agreed. I even handed in my notice at work. That's why I'm temping now. That dinner was supposed to be a celebration, but he said it was reckless. We rowed about it.'

'Well, sure,' Annie said soothingly. 'Sure it's a risk, but it's a calculated risk. That's different.'

'I lost my nerve,' I said, frowning at hearing myself saying these words. 'I wanted him to be pleased, but he wasn't. Then he finished with me, saying I was a fool and I ought to know better.'

The words still hurt. Holding the telephone under my chin, with my finger curled around the cord, I watched the dust motes dance in the shafts of sunlight. The sky outside was a deep blue; the plant I had saved was growing stronger, the brown leaves replaced by beautiful, glossy green buds.

The next day, Annie rang back.

'I've been thinking,' she said. 'We both need cheering up. I'm going to bring you lunch.'

Annie arrived at one o'clock. I was a little nervous, but when I saw her from the window, wearing a large straw hat and a floaty pale dress, hints of dark hair poking out from under the brim, and when I opened the door and saw her amused, kind face, I knew all would be well.

We both laughed.

'This is crazy,' she said, looking around the offices. 'Does the phone ring much?'

'No.' I smiled at her. 'It's mostly been you.'

Annie brought the most luxurious picnic with her and laid it out on the floor of the front office. There were warm baguettes, a range of cheeses, sweet peaches – their skins blushed and furry, two different salads and a small, lopsided chocolate cake. She had also brought a tiny bunch of sweet peas, which she put in a mug we found in the kitchen and popped on top of the switchboard.

As there was only one chair, we sat on the floor, smiling at each other, and as we ate the food we talked as though we were already old friends.

'I love sweet peas.' She nodded at the flowers. ' "Here are sweet peas, on tiptoe for a flight, with wings of gentle flush . . ." I can't remember the rest, it's a poem. Will you have them in your flower shop? I think you should.'

I felt a shot of happiness then, a liquid delight falling on my skin with the sunshine.

'I think I should too,' I said, biting into a peach. 'You're so right.'

And we both grinned, at my decision and at this spontaneous friendship, which seemed to have come from nowhere.

Later, we packed up the picnic things and picked the crumbs off the floor, feeling rebellious and pleased with ourselves.

As Annie made to go, she turned to me and said,

'Do you know what sweet peas are meant to represent? Delicate, blissful pleasure. Oh, and they also mean – goodbye and thank you for a lovely time.'

This summer, I have sweet peas sitting in a vast tin bucket at the front of the shop, a delicate tumble of deliciously fragrant, wild-stemmed joy. They remind me of that summer afternoon when everything felt paused and difficult, and how my accidental friend showed me the odd pleasures that life might offer you when it's least expected. That's why they make me happy, because it was that afternoon I was given the confidence again to hope and dare.

The Naked Truth

BY WENDY HOLDEN

*P*eople these days talk a lot about reinvention. They get life coaches and leave jobs in the civil service to take up cheese-making in Guernsey. Or they kick over the housewifely traces to fulfil a lifetime's urge to be a trapeze artist.

I'd always fancied doing something different too. I was good at drawing as a child. So was Picasso, of course, but from there our paths diverged. Pablo didn't go to typing college, marry an accountant and clock up twenty-five years as a secretary in a Midlands widgets firm.

My husband Stephen didn't exactly encourage my creative side. He was risk-averse in most areas of life and, in particular, self-expression. Instead of paintings, which he feared might reveal something embarrassing about us, throughout our marriage he hung framed photos on our walls instead. Personally, I felt they revealed much more; the one of our own wedding, for example, advertised the carbuncle Stephen had had on the day, also how fat and plain I'd been. The gawky school photographs of the children illustrated Toby's unfortunate teeth (since corrected) and Alice's even more unfortunate rebel phase with the nose stud and shaved eyebrows. Worst of all, in pride of place and blown up to blurring point, was the picture of Stephen looking embarrassingly sycophantic as Princess Anne toured the company offices.

Stephen was an accountant the whole of our married life; to say he lacked spontaneity is putting it mildly. On holiday, he rarely wanted to go anywhere other than Wales, and was so mean he made me use teabags twice. So when, in the grip of a midlife crisis, he left me after thirty years, you could say it was a surprise.

In his farewell address to me, he explained he felt it was his last chance to grab life by the balls – an inapt choice of words given that The Other Woman was an office manager with hair rather longer and brassier than seemed advisable for her age. I felt oddly neutral about it all. Part of me even felt sorry for her. I hoped she liked Caernarfon and PG tips without the kick.

My main sensation, however, was of a lid being lifted. I felt I knew how the butter must feel when the top is taken off the tub and it stares up, blinking, into the bright lights of the fridge. I suppose I must have loved Stephen once, but I can't say I remember exactly when. Maybe between seven and ten o'clock one October night in 1975.

The bombshell of divorce was quickly followed by the bombshell of Mr Shufflebottom, head of our widgets firm since God was a lad, dropping dead on the golf course. For a wobbly few weeks it looked as if Shufflebottom, Sidecrank & Shufflebottom, Est. 1936, might go to the wall, but then the news came that a distant, London-based relation was to take over. In the meantime, stringent economic measures were taken. Shifts were slashed and instead of the forty hours a week I had been used to, I found myself in possession of a part-time job.

The children were appalled.

'You can't work part-time, Mum,' they objected, no doubt thinking of the nest egg they imagined I was building up for them.

As Toby does something freelance and precarious in computers, and Alice is a stay-at-home mum whose child benefit has been slashed, they're rather depending on me. They know better than to ask for anything from their father. But I failed to see why I should remain the breadwinner when my children left home ten years ago.

No, I was going to do something for myself. New clothes, high heels, having my hair cut and coloured, and having a makeover in the John Lewis beauty hall: that was only the start of it. Then – then – I was going to go on an art course.

I was after something mild with watercolours, but for some reason such classes were few and far between. The courses at the local further education institutes all seemed very directional. There were opportunities galore if you wanted to make sculptures out of offal or work in neon, but simple painting was hard to come by. Goodness knows how Van Gogh, Leonardo and the rest would have managed if they were trying to start off in the Wolverhampton of 2010.

'There's one place left on our life class,' I was told by the information officer of the last place I called. He sounded doubtful.

Life classes? Naked people? Me?

I felt shocked at first, but then the idea took hold. Why not? Drawing the human form is, after all, one of the building blocks of art training. Also, I liked the idea of a life class. Coming back to life, in my case. A new life.

By the time I went to the first session, which was held in the local primary school, I'd got over the idea of contemplating a naked woman for two hours. I'd even practised insouciant expressions in the mirror. It helped that the rest of the class seemed very relaxed. It was a wide social mix: a couple of teenagers chewing their hair, an intense man with a beard and a couple of grey-haired ladies, one of whom I recognised from behind the counter of the local library.

Clutching the pads and pencils we'd been asked to bring, we sat in a semicircle around a chaise longue covered in a white sheet. A vague-looking woman with frizzy blonde hair came hurrying in, whom I assumed to be the model, but she turned out to be the art teacher.

Then the model arrived and started, in brisk and businesslike fashion, to get undressed. I could hardly look; I wanted to be anywhere else. While I was now quite relaxed about nudity, it was female nudity I was anticipating. The thought that the model would be a man had simply never occurred to me.

And such a handsome man too. Broad-shouldered, long-legged, dark-haired, with a hairy – but not too hairy – chest. And rather wicked eyes.

I swallowed involuntarily.

I could hardly look – but forced myself to – as he undid his shirt buttons and matter-of-factly dropped his boxer shorts. Then he arranged himself on the sheeted chaise as if it were the most natural thing in the world. As he caught my eye, I wildly scanned the school walls with their papier mâché models of the solar system and elementary pleasantries in French.

I noticed that no one else seemed to think he was Adonis incarnate. The rest of the class were composedly drawing. My pencil alone skittered across the page in a jagged line reminiscent of a heart monitor. Determinedly, I chose the least controversial body part to look at – the sole of his foot – and applied my B2 with a vengeance.

'Very good,' murmured the teacher, pausing behind me. 'Feet are terribly difficult to draw.'

Actually, in terms of the man before me, I could think of more difficult areas. Glancing over at the librarian, I was startled to see she was rendering just that with the sang-froid of someone drawing a cucumber. The funny thing is that, by the end of the two-hour session, I was doing the same.

At the end we all packed up and left as matter-of-factly as if we'd spent two hours stuffing envelopes. The model dressed and left without a word, which I imagined was the convention on such occasions. It made sense; it would be odd to hang around and chat when people had been staring at your privates for two hours.

I returned to work the next morning feeling like an entirely different woman. The best way to describe it was emancipated. I imagined it must be because my creative side had had an airing.

The following week I returned to the art class and was able to render the model's muscled posterior with only the occasional flutter. I seemed to be attaining some degree of self-control. You could almost call it confidence. But not confidence in my abilities as an artist. It had been obvious from the first session that I was never going to be any more than average at it.

No, the creativity that had been unleashed in me was in terms of business. All of a sudden, I was having an unstoppable, unprecedented stream of ideas. At work, taking a genuine interest for the first time, I had effortlessly spotted some areas where widget making could be done more efficiently. I planned to discuss my thoughts with the new owner when he made an appearance, but he was yet to visit the factory. One couldn't help sensing a certain lack of enthusiasm on his part.

I was distracted at this point from both art and world widget domination by some cracks in my kitchen ceiling. Then a drip started under the sink, and a damp patch started to spread across the hall wall. Rebuilding my life I may have been, but my home was clearly falling apart. It was the first time since he had left that I actually missed Stephen; he had always Done It Himself in order to avoid Opening His Wallet.

In the light of that, it felt both thrilling and daring to run my finger down the 'Builders' section of the local free-sheet small ads, find someone who sounded likely and invite the answerphone to send him round to my address.

My doorbell rang within the hour. As I opened up, my smile of amazed and grateful greeting changed to an 'O' of horror.

It was the naked man from the life class. Clothed now, of course. Yet, knowing as I did what lay beneath his stonewashed jeans, white T-shirt and even those little beige boots that builders always wear, I felt my face sizzle with shame. He, on the other hand, seemed perfectly relaxed.

'Ah,' he said, looking pleased. 'It's you.'

I now realised the real reason he had never spoken in the classes. English was not his first language.

Taking command of the situation immediately, he walked past me into the hall and began squinting up into the cornices. He shook his head, sucked his teeth and looked up at me with those eyes I knew so disturbingly well.

'Who paints this?' he demanded, grimacing.

'My husband,' I confessed. 'But he has gone,' I

added hurriedly, meeting the other man's quizzical expression. 'He no longer lives here.'

'Is good thing,' he pronounced. 'Because this ceiling is rubbish. He miss, miss, miss.'

As he gestured upwards, I remembered Stephen wobbling on the ladder, inexpertly wielding his roller. Yes, he had missed, missed, missed, and in more ways than one.

'I start now,' the builder said, politely edging past me to the front door through which I could see a neat white van parked by the roadside. 'You need lot of work,' he remarked as he came back with a toolbox under one brawny arm and a tin of paint in the other. He flashed me a grin that made my heart turn over.

'Yes,' I agreed, with a soaring feeling inside. 'A lot of work.'

The next Monday morning, I walked to the office with a spring in my step. Over the weekend, Jan – as I discovered was his name – had made a start on my refurbishment and made me happier in two days than Stephen had managed in two decades.

Now, once again, it was time to think widgets. Before I could persuade myself not to do it, I sat down at my desk, opened my email and typed a long, detailed memo to the absentee chairman, setting out my ideas about increasing productivity.

There was no immediate response, and I spent an uncomfortable couple of days expecting dismissal. Then the phone rang.

'You gave me a pretty stripped-down take on the

situation,' remarked the chairman as he offered me the position of regional manager.

'Yes,' I agreed as I accepted. 'But the naked truth is always better, don't you think?'

Four Days to Christmas

BY CATHY KELLY

*F*our days before Christmas, Vicky Ryan stood in the supermarket with her list in her hand and misery in her heart. She had just four days in which to finish cleaning the house from top to bottom and to force herself into some semblance of festive cheer. It was hard to know which was going to be harder.

She wheeled her trolley tiredly round the aisles. More crackers, just in case. There were going to be fourteen at lunch, after all. Gluten-free mince pies for Aunt Phyllis, who had a delicate stomach.

Aunt Phyllis had been coming to Vicky and Mike's for Christmas for almost as long as they'd been married, twenty years at least. The only time ninety-year-old Aunt Phyllis forgot about her digestive system was when she was into her fifth Irish coffee.

Must check if we have enough drink, Vicky reminded herself.

When her mother died, Vicky had taken over as the sensible, organised person who hosted Christmas, kept up with all the far-flung relatives and remembered family anniversaries. Everyone in the extended family loved her Christmas lunch.

'You have that magic touch for cooking and decorating,' her sister-in-law once said, admiring the hall festooned with ivy garlands and gingham Santas.

The guest list had grown every year. This year, apart from Phyllis and Vicky's sister, Sasha, there was Mike's sister and her whole family. Not to mention that nice Canadian doctor who was working as a locum in Mike's GP practice.

Once, Vicky had loved doing it. Christmas was such a magical time and she'd wanted it to be memorable for her beloved son, Anton.

'Thank you for making it all so special,' Mike had said so many times in the crisp dawn of Christmas morning, when Anton would be delightedly showing off Santa's goodies.

This would be the first year they'd have Christmas without Anton. Twenty-one and on a gap year in Australia, he wasn't coming home.

'It's too expensive, Mum,' he'd said on one of his weekly Skype calls. 'Unless you want to send me the money . . .'

Vicky knew she had to let go. A good mother had to give her children both roots and wings, even though she'd have mortgaged her soul to see him.

'We'll be fine,' she said, outwardly smiling. 'You'll have a marvellous time there.'

When she'd hung up, she'd burst into tears.

Mike hadn't put his arms around her, the way he once would have.

'He's got to fly the nest, love,' he'd muttered somewhat absently, before going back to his medical journal.

At that moment, Vicky had felt her heart break. It was as if she'd lost both of them – Anton and Mike.

In the supermarket, she suddenly caught sight of herself reflected in the door of a freezer cabinet.

A tired forty-nine-year-old with greying roots stared back at her. She worked on the reception desk in Mike's practice and hadn't managed to get time off to have her hair dyed. It looked as dreadful as she felt.

In her chic, glossy apartment, Sasha stared glumly at her haul of Christmas presents and wished she wasn't going to her sister's for Christmas lunch. She loved Vicky so much, but she also hated Christmas. It was for families: not your family of origin, but for the new one you'd made, ideally a husband and kids. None of which Sasha had. When you were single at forty-five, the ideal Christmas was on a beach somewhere far away from the madness.

Next year, she promised herself, she'd go the Caribbean.

Mike Ryan put down the phone and sat silently in his surgery. He shouldn't have been shocked to hear that this patient had died. The tumour had been inoperable. But Lisa had been such a vital woman, so full of life.

She'd reminded him of Vicky. The same courage and humour, the same warm-heartedness. It was the resemblance between Lisa and his wife that made Lisa's death feel so raw.

He'd learned to distance himself but even though he had been a GP for twenty-three years, some deaths still touched home. What would he do if anything happened to Vicky?

Things hadn't been great between them since Anton had left. The empty-nest syndrome had hit her like a tornado.

Mike was aware that he hadn't tried hard enough to understand what she was going through. It was ironic, he knew, that a man could be so loved by his women patients for his listening abilities, yet not really listen to his wife.

But in his defence, Mike was used to Vicky being the strong one. She was the one who'd supported him financially during the early years of the practice. She was the one who'd taken part-time jobs, who'd made every Christmas fabulous using limited funds and her creative ability to transform the house into a welcoming sanctuary.

It was startling to see the effect that Anton's leaving home had had on her.

On the surface, it was as if she was no longer the young, beautiful, dark-haired girl he'd fallen in love with. And yet that girl was still there.

With a shock, Mike realised the problem was that he never bothered to reach out to Vicky any more.

He loved his wife so much. Why didn't he tell Vicky that? Or show her?

By noon on Christmas Day, the guests had started to arrive.

Aunt Phyllis had turned vegetarian.

'Forgot to tell you, dear.' She beamed at Vicky.

Sasha came next, red-eyed.

'Sorry,' she said, hugging her sister. 'Just feel a bit miserable, that's all.'

The phone rang loudly and Vicky retreated to the kitchen to answer it, wondering how she was going to cope with a whole day of this.

In the kitchen, Mike was holding the phone, a look of love on his face that Vicky didn't think she'd seen for a very long time.

'It's Anton,' he said.

'It's midnight there, I thought you'd be asleep,' said Vicky into the phone and began to cry.

'The party's only just starting,' Anton said cheerfully. 'I had to phone 'cos I got Dad's email about you two coming to Australia in January. I can't wait . . .'

'Mike.' Vicky clamped one hand over the mouthpiece. She knew how tight money was. 'We can't afford this,' she began.

Mike stepped forward to hold her closely, the phone nestled between them.

'It's not about money,' he said softly. 'It's about us. I wanted to give you something precious for Christmas to show you how much I love you.'

Vicky's tears fell but they were happy ones.

'Mum, Dad,' came Anton's muffled voice on the phone. 'This is a terrible line . . .'

In the dining room, Sasha found a tall, dark man peering at the family photos on the wall. He turned as she came in and a smile lit up his face.

Despite herself, Sasha smiled back.

'What part of the family are you?' he asked, holding his hand out, still smiling.

'I'm the unmarried sister,' said Sasha, grinning.

His smile widened.

'I'm the unmarried doctor they took pity on.'

'Best if we sit together,' Sasha said gravely. 'Otherwise, Aunt Phyllis will give you her entire medical history. I'll save you.'

Their eyes met.

'I think I'd like that,' he said.

Sonata d'Eté

BY DOUGLAS KENNEDY

*B*ack then, I fell in love far too easily. Back then, I didn't have the first idea what love was. Back then, I was simply hungry for experience – and far too unworldly when it came to understanding that life occasionally presents you with a decisive moment, on which hinges the entire trajectory of future events.

I digress. It was the summer of 1975. I was twenty. I had just spent a year studying at the Royal College of Music – where I was in composition classes and was writing my first string quartet: very atonal and Boulezian, very out there. I had just spent six months with the first serious girlfriend in my life and had discovered a weakness for Irish women that would (in years to come) carry me into a fifteen-year marriage with someone who – as she admitted to me in its dying moments – never particularly liked me.

But all that was decades in front of me: the future that none of us can ever discern, as life has this intriguing habit of running according to a script that is as random as it is unpredictable. At the time I was twenty. I had, with great regret, returned to the United

States after ten months of louche bohemian living in London – an experience that had happily corrupted me. It had also made me realise that the success ethic, which had been drilled into me from a young age, was a trap that would ensnare me and keep me in a safe profession in a life I already knew I didn't want.

But, again, I digress. I returned to the States because I had a summer job in Maine – as the administrative assistant on a summer festival of classical music. Just before leaving London I'd broken up with my Irish girlfriend, who was named Anne. And on the third day of my work week – the day when all the musicians arrived – I met another Ann, though she spelled her first name without an 'e'. Like me she was a New Yorker. Like me she was twenty. And upon first seeing her lugging her cello from the administrative building to the hall of residence where she'd be sleeping for the next six weeks, I immediately approached her and offered to carry her instrument for her.

Yes, that was a tactical move on my part – because I was already smitten with her. She could best be described as willowy. Tall and willowy – with flowing blonde hair and skin that was translucent (could skin be that perfect?). She was dressed in a gossamer skirt that, in the honeyed glow of a New England summer morning, showed off her long legs. She was wearing a white embroidered shirt – and I remember immediately thinking that this was the New York bohemian girl of my dreams – and one who played the cello to boot.

Not only did she play the cello, she was gifted. A student at Juilliard – America's premier conservatory – she was described by the director of the music festival as a musician to watch: a serious talent with serious intelligence.

But what I remember most of all about Ann at the outset was her mixture of worldliness and innocence. She was wildly knowledgeable about books and music. We spent hours talking about new novels and new music: whether the Shostakovich quartets were better than Bartók, Ellington versus Count Basie, Updike versus Cheever, the cello sonatas of Brahms, whether twelve-tone music would last out the century, and why Haydn was the great underestimated composer of the classical age.

The conversation was always animated – with me being the intellectual show-off (well, that was my style back then) and Ann always sounding more thoughtful, more considered. I loved that about her. Just as I loved the way her smile was always couched in a certain wistfulness – a hint that, for all her outward optimism (as Ann herself told me, she preferred to see the glass half full and life as an enterprise full of possibility), she also had a wistful side to her. She would cry easily in bad movies and during certain passages of music (the slow movements of the Brahms sonatas would always get her). She would cry after making love, which we did at every moment that summer when we could sneak back to one of our respective rooms and throw our clothes off and devour each other with abandon.

It was an astonishing two months. I was with someone who not only could challenge me intellectually, who knew so much about the things that so interested me, who wanted to hear all the small compositions I had written to date (while also gently encouraging me to stop writing just astringent music and perhaps consider something marginally lyrical and accessible), but who also genuinely loved me. She told me this for the first time as the summer drew to a close, as she was about to return to Juilliard in New York and I was to start my final year at university.

'You know, my parents have been together since they were twenty . . . and that's over a quarter of a century ago. And the thing is: as my mom told me a few years back, the moment she saw my father she knew that he was it. Her destiny. And that's what I felt when I first saw you.'

I didn't react well to this comment – as sweetly rendered and loving as it so evidently was. The part of me that feared entrapment – that looked upon marital life as a replication of my parents' endlessly combustible marriage – suddenly flinched at this glimpse of a domestic future. Ann saw this and put her arms around me and reassured me that she wasn't trying to trap me; that, on the contrary, she was willing to wait if I wanted to buzz off to Paris and study for a year, or if I didn't feel like getting married until we were both twenty-five.

'I don't want you to feel under pressure,' she told

me, all quiet and loving. 'I just want you to know that, for me, you are the man of my life.'

I went back to university – and, in the weeks after Ann's declaration, I slept with any woman who would have me. Every second weekend I would take the Greyhound bus down to New York and stay with Ann at her hall of residence near Columbia University. We would make love half the weekend, our times out of bed spent going to concerts on student tickets or hearing alumni of the Ellington band at their weekly jam session at the West End Café.

The weekends were never less than wonderful. Ann never mentioned 'our future' again. But the part of me that always expected difficulties – since family life with my parents and brothers was nothing but non-stop difficulties – couldn't quite accept her decency, her calmness, the fact that she could actually do 'nice'. So I kept sleeping with as many women as I could at university – and I kept Ann at a certain distance.

The year passed. I won a fellowship in composition at IRCAM in Paris. Ann was so thrilled for me – and said that her teacher at Juilliard had a colleague at the Conservatoire de Paris who would be willing to take her on as a student for a year.

'Just think: we can find some cheap garret,' she told me, 'and learn French and be together and tell our children years from now about our year in Paris. It will be wonderful.'

'Yes,' I told her. 'It will be wonderful.'

I was supposed to see her the following weekend. But when the Greyhound bus stopped in Boston I got off and called a woman I knew at Radcliffe: a casual fuck buddy (even though this expression was never used back then) to ask if I might share her bed for a few days.

'I've got nothing else to do,' she said.

All during the weekend I hated myself for standing Ann up, for not even having the simple courtesy to call her and say I was not coming down. But the other part of me – the part that could not accept her decency, her love for me – told me it was best this way. Best to let her see what a selfish bastard I was, not worthy of her affections. So I never made the call, and spent the two days smoking dope and carousing with my Radcliffe friend, who looked upon me as a convenience, nothing more.

Then, at the end of the weekend, I returned to university. As this was a time long before mobile phones or the Internet, it was easy not to have your movements traced – and when I got back to the little apartment I had off campus, I found a note from the local police station, asking me to give them a call. Expecting the worst, I picked up the phone and found out from the sergeant on the front desk that a Ms Ann Somerville had been so frantic about my whereabouts all weekend, so certain I had been abducted or mowed down by a car, that she had called the local cops to see if they knew whether I was alive or dead.

'Seems you've got a lady who really cares about you,'

the cop on duty told me, his voice full of sarcastic reproach. 'Why don't you be the gent and call her back, tell her you're not dead. It's the least you owe her.'

So I did just that. Ann was so relieved to hear from me, so happy that I was safe and well, that I had no choice but to tell her the truth: that I had been sharing someone else's bed all weekend, that this Radcliffe cutie was around the tenth woman I'd slept with in the last month, that I didn't show up because—

But by that time the phone had gone dead. I stared at the receiver for a good five minutes, asking myself why I had been so cruel, so vindictive, so despicable.

I never heard from Ann Somerville again. Nor did I know much about her whereabouts for twenty years.

By that time my year-long fellowship in Paris was ancient history. I was a professor of composition at Indiana University – which, though it might be one of the best conservatories in the country, was still stuck out in the middle of the corn belt, a long way from the Manhattan of my childhood or the life I once envisaged for myself as a composer in a major metropolis. Instead I was an academic – and one who composed only occasionally.

My wife, Maeve, was a one-time promising soprano from Cork, now a mother of two and an increasingly cold and belligerent woman who closely resembled my mother when it came to her dissatisfaction with life and her emotional distance from me. Life with Maeve had turned into an ongoing source of displeasure – and

I knew that I would have to hit the eject button soon, as costly and ghastly as that would be.

And then in 1999, out of nowhere, came an article in the *New York Times* about a cellist named Ann Somerville who, after a quiet career as a musician, was suddenly in the news after stepping in at the last moment for an ailing Mstislav Rostropovich during a New York Philharmonic concert. Like me, she was forty-two at the time. Unlike me, she was – so the article stated – 'happily married for twenty-one years to David Monroe – now the head of the piano division at Juilliard'.

It went on: 'I met David at Juilliard around three weeks after my first serious boyfriend dumped me. We've been together ever since.'

I tossed the newspaper away. I sat down and wrote a letter that I never sent: a letter in which I told Ann Somerville that I had been a fool; that I had bypassed her because I couldn't 'do happy'; that I had chosen someone who couldn't 'do nice' as a wife and had been paying the price since then; and that not a day went by when I didn't think of her and wonder why I had been so absurd, so self-sabotaging, so determined to push away the one woman in my life to date who loved me. And in conclusion I wrote this:

'It occurs to me that, after forty-two years, I still understand very little about why we do the things we do. But I do know this: I will regret what I did for the rest of my life.'

Of course I never sent the letter. When Ann – now

suddenly a celebrated cellist – gave a recital at the university six months later, I sat in the back of the hall, my head hung low, unable to look at this still-beautiful woman as she negotiated her way brilliantly through three of Brahms's sonatas.

Of course I couldn't go backstage afterwards. Of course I knew I was being a coward. But, then again, I had always been a coward about such things. And I wondered: was my story that unique? Don't we often sidestep felicity and embrace that which will eventually damage us? Is it so hard for us to accept happiness?

I have no answers to those questions. But upon returning home that night – after hearing the woman I had purposefully lost play Brahms and find, within his work, the aching melancholy that seemed to haunt my own life – I packed a bag and walked out. Maeve could not believe I had the audacity to finally leave her. She threatened to ruin me professionally and financially.

'Be my guest,' I said. 'Because I ruined my life the day I married you.'

'There's someone else, isn't there?' she challenged.

I nodded, knowing this would be the death-knell of our marriage, of everything between us. Maeve was horrified and furious.

'And how long has this been going on?'

'Twenty-two years.'

'But we've been together for nineteen of those years. You've been carrying on with someone else for all that time.'

I could have explained that, until tonight, I hadn't laid eyes on Ann Somerville since 1977. I could have informed her that I had always regretted destroying her love for me, and that I now realised she was everything I had ever wanted. I could have said that she had been happily married for the past twenty-two years and was probably unaware of my existence. But instead I simply fell silent.

Maeve – for whom life was an endless argument – reacted with even more rage, calling me a series of scatological names, telling me that when she was through with me I would have no career and no friends. I just shrugged and said nothing.

'Stop the silent act, you bastard,' she yelled. 'And tell me straight to my face that you still love this little bitch of a cellist. Come on, you arse. Tell me you love her.'

I met her vindictive gaze. I said: 'I love her.'

Then I picked up my bag and headed to the door. As I left Maeve yelled: 'You're about to lose everything.'

I turned back and uttered the last line I would say to her, outside that which was transmitted between us by lawyers.

'I lost everything years ago.'

Christmas List

BY SOPHIE KINSELLA

17 August

O K. This year I'm organised. It's the middle of August and I've already done my Christmas shopping.

My plan is simple yet brilliant. Everyone will receive the same thing: a handmade pottery bowl from the Spanish market. I've got ten of them stashed on the back seat of the car, safely done up in bubble wrap.

No frantically flicking through novelty catalogues for me. No braving Oxford Street in the rain. And you can't go wrong with a pottery bowl, can you?

They had men's wallets at the market too. Hand-tooled in leather, with a divine scent, all woody and sensual. I picked one up and breathed it in. It's the kind of present I would have bought Chris. Chestnut brown to match his eyes. If he'd been here with me, as he was supposed to be . . .

And then my eyes rushed with tears and I couldn't answer the Spanish stallholder. Stupid eyes. Stupid wallet. Stupid man.

I wonder if he's been thinking about me. In his igloo in Norway.

Or whatever they have in Norway.

Then Anne came rushing up, brandishing three bikinis she'd got for ten euros, and hustled me off for a cocktail. If she noticed my tears, she didn't say anything. She's been good like that, this holiday. In fact, I've already decided to give her one of the bowls for Christmas.

26 August

Bloody bubble wrap. Four of the bowls broke on the way back from Spain. Four. I blame Anne, wedging that crate of wine in at the last moment. Still, never mind. I've got six. And Christmas is months away.

5 September

Alex and David's party last night. Only a couple of people mentioned Chris, and I managed to smile and shrug.

I'd forgotten it was their anniversary till I glanced at the invitation on the way out. But it was OK: I gave them a pottery bowl. Five left. I'm still ahead of the game. I'll just have to buy a few extras.

12 September

I've bought Mum a picnic set for Christmas. Really smart, with china plates and real glasses. Just enough for two.

There was a huge hamper for sale in the shop too, all wicker and leather straps, with room for wine bottles. Chris would have loved it. We had so many picnics in the early days. Nothing fancy, just an M&S bag of goodies, a rug, a bottle of wine. Lying all afternoon in the sun until the shadows crept over us.

Anyway. That was then.

16 September

Mum's birthday. Dad gave her a bloody picnic set. I couldn't believe it.

17 September

It's fine, I'll just reorganise my list. I'll give the picnic set to my brother. The pottery bowls can go to Mum, Dad, Granny, Grandpa and Anne.

I still need to get presents for the two nephews, my sister and my hairdresser. And my boss. But it's OK. Christmas is ages away. I'm still ahead of the game.

2 *October*

Big day. Packing up. I'm moving out of the flat tomorrow. It's too big for one.

It was different when I was with Chris. He works from home, so his presence was always there. His papers, his coffee cups, his strange scientific data everywhere. We'd be talking and his eyes would take on that milky look and I'd know he was thinking about numbers. I used to get jealous. I wanted him to be here, with me, not with them.

Now of course I realise numbers are just part of him, like his hair or his skin. When I picture him now, he's sitting on the edge of a snowy vista, dressed in his North Face parka, communing with his numbers.

I wonder what Norwegian numbers are like.

4 *October*

The removers broke two of my Spanish pottery bowls. I was so livid, I pretended the sugar had run out.

The girl from the company said, 'If you supply us with receipts, we'll send you a cheque and you can get replacements.'

I explained about the tiny Spanish market in the hills and the man with his leather apron and the stall piled high with handmade bowls.

She suggested I went to Ikea.

7 October

This is beyond a joke. The glasses in the picnic set have smashed too. And the company can't supply replacements until the New Year.

I'll give my brother something else. Maybe a bowl.

15 October

Mum: bowl (?)
Dad: bowl (?)
Anne: bowl (?)

22 October

I'm losing confidence in the bowls. I got them out and looked at them again. Somehow they looked different in the Spanish sunshine. Less garish.

Maybe I should flip through some of those novelty Christmas catalogues.

25 October

Mum: novelty pillow set
Dad: novelty torch

Nephews: don't know yet. I've spent all evening circling things in marker and trying to pay online.

There was a catalogue from a literary book club, selling beautiful hardbacks. Before I could stop myself I'd spent half an hour mentally buying presents for Chris. Histories of mathematicians. Explanations of the world. That's all Chris wants to do, explain the world.

He can painstakingly analyse some tiny piece of weather system and reduce it to numbers. He can interpret the clouds. But when it comes to himself he doesn't have the first idea.

26 October

He said he didn't think we could sustain a long-distance relationship. He said we had enough communication problems when we were in the same room. And then he said he was definitely going to Norway.

Nephews: novelty Frisbees. Perfect.

27 October

What I should have said to Chris is that communication isn't about distance. It's about wanting to hear. These days, you can be on the other side of the world and still listening to the person you love.

I suppose the truth is, I wasn't sure if he was the person I loved. You know, the one.

And he wasn't sure either. Which is why we let each other go.

3 November

The novelty Frisbees are sold out. I've tried fifteen websites. Who are all these bloody people buying Frisbees?

Finally I got through to a work-experience boy in Solihull. He promised to bike two Frisbees to me tomorrow.

7 November

Anne came and dragged me off for a drink. She said I was getting obsessional about Christmas shopping and I'd been at it since August and she was worried.

Then she said, 'I know what this is. It's displacement so you don't have to think about Chris. Isn't it?'

I said, 'I don't know what you're talking about,' and stirred my mojito.

Then she said, 'Look, you're stressing too much about these presents. Why not just buy the same thing for everyone and have done with it?'

I almost yelled at her, 'I tried that!'

15 November

Email from my sister: 'The boys would adore camping equipment, if you haven't bought anything already.'

Maybe Dad would like a Frisbee. Or perhaps my hairdresser would.

22 November

A new guy has moved in downstairs. He came to borrow an adaptor and looked at all my boxes still lining the hall.

'Just moved in too?'

His name's Adrian. He's a physio and has weirdly developed calf muscles.

26 November

Adrian has volunteered to help me with my boxes. He's coming round tonight. He said he'd bring the Doritos.

Does that mean I'm supplying the drinks? What do physios drink, anyway? Should I get Lucozade Sport? Protein shakes?

I'll get some wine too.

1 December

He didn't touch the wine. He drank low-alcohol beer, which he brought himself.

Then, at the end of the evening he put the empty bottles in the new 'Glass Recycling' box that is standing in the corner of my hall, labelled with a Post-It. Adrian brought the Post-Its too. Everywhere I look, I can see instructions in strangely girly writing: 'Paper Recycling'. 'Admin'. 'Cosmetics (unopened)'.

He said he could tell I needed a system. He said it was hard, moving on. He said he'd split up with his university sweetheart a year ago. All this while he was unpacking, flattening boxes. He even sorted everything out into bin bags and humped them down the stairs for me.

I said nothing much. I get the feeling he's used to silent people. I imagine a series of patients in his office, in pain, wanting someone to give them the answer.

8 December

My Christmas presents have gone! Vanished! I've searched the flat again and again. All I've found is one Spanish bowl. How on earth can a whole box of presents disappear—

Oh my God. No.

No.

12 December

Adrian was mortified, offered to pay and everything. I couldn't get angry, though. He's been so helpful.

He asked me what my Christmas plans were. Did I want to join him or was I going back home to Devon?

I coughed and mumbled. Didn't commit either way.

17 December

The novelty cushions are out of stock. And the novelty torches. And there's a postal strike. I'll have to take an afternoon off work.

On the plus side, it's snowing.

20 December

Adrian has left under my door an invitation to dinner on Christmas Day.

22 December

Six hours trekking up and down Oxford Street. I'm a wreck. My feet hurt, my ears are ringing, my hands are red and frozen, after I left my gloves somewhere. Maybe in the Selfridges men's department.

I bought Dad cufflinks, then saw a beautiful sheep-skin coat on display. I couldn't help lingering by it. Chestnut brown.

Anyway. Move on. Don't dwell. It's time to sit down with a mulled wine, I've bought the sachets.

Oh God. The doorbell. Adrian knows I'm in. Am I going to his place for Christmas or not? Do I dare ignore it?

24 December

I didn't ignore it. I swung the door open, already rehearsing excuses, wondering if I should feign illness.

And there he was, filling the doorway. North Face parka. Chestnut eyes. A smattering of snow on his shoulders.

'I was Christmas shopping,' he said. 'In Oslo.'

I stared dumbly back, feeling totally surreal. Chris. Here on my doorstep. The only thing I could think was that he hasn't yet picked up a Norwegian accent.

'Me too,' I said at last. 'I was shopping too. Although not in Oslo. Obviously.'

'The only person I wanted to buy anything for was you.' His voice was gruff. 'The only person I could think about was you.'

His eyes were burning into mine and I could see the question in them: *am I too late?*

I gave a tiny, non-committal shrug. Maybe he was.

Maybe my future lay with Adrian and low-alcohol beer.

'That's very sweet. Actually, I haven't really given you a thought,' I lied. 'I'm very busy these days.'

'I know I've messed up. I know you've moved on.'

His eyes looked past me at the flat. I could see him reading the Post-It notes in puzzlement.

'But you have to know: I'm sorry. I've done a lot of thinking, over there. You were right. About us. About everything.'

And there it was. My Christmas present.

'Can I . . . come in at least?' His face was humble and hopeful. 'Could we talk? Is there a way forward?'

I tortured him a few moments longer.

'I haven't got you anything,' I said at last. 'So if you're expecting a present you'll be disappointed.'

'No I won't.'

His arms were already round me. I could feel the chill of his jacket, could taste the snow on his cheek.

Then he turned and reached for a wheelie case, and I blinked in amazement. It was stuffed with presents. Gift-wrapped boxes, all the colours of the rainbow.

25 December

It's just gone midnight. Christmas Day is a few seconds old. I've left Chris asleep in bed and tiptoed to the living room. My tiny tree is twinkling away, with all the rainbow presents underneath.

And I'm wrapping up my present to him. A hand-made Spanish pottery bowl.

A Small Adventure

BY SANTA MONTEFIORE

*A*my trudged through the woods, hands in pockets, head tucked into her hood. Summer rain fell in a light drizzle so that the leaves glistened on the trees and cobwebs were exposed in their bejewelled splendour.

Birds chorused in the highest branches and Amy's heart should have sung with them, but it felt as heavy as her mud-coated boots.

So this was her life? In her late forties, with children grown up and a husband busy at work, travelling so much he was rarely at home – and, when he was, she felt more like a domestic than a wife, cooking, washing and ironing in a monotonous cycle. Did she love him? If she did, it was a familiar love that was barely aware of itself.

She trudged on, gazing bleakly into her future. Was this as good as it was going to get?

When she got home she made a cup of tea and sat at the kitchen table to read the papers. She should have been an art teacher, she thought, remembering how she had given up working in the local school after she had had children. But how could she inspire children now? She had lost her imagination somewhere on her journey, along with her sense of fun.

The telephone rang and she sensed it was John calling to say he'd be home late. She picked it up and answered flatly.

'Eloise!'

Amy was surprised to hear the familiar voice ringing down the line from America. It had been months since she had last spoken to her old best friend from university. Eloise had gone straight from Exeter to New York to work for an art dealer, and had then married him, given birth to three boys and divorced ten years later, keeping in touch through it all.

'I'm getting married!'

'Again?'

'Yes, but it's different this time. It's Big Love, honey.'

She even sounded American now.

'Who is he?'

'I can't wait for you to meet him. I miss you, Amy! God dammit, no one makes me laugh like you do. Please say you'll come to the wedding. It's only small, just my very good friends at his house on Harbor Island. We're getting married on the beach! Bring John. It's very romantic.'

The words 'John' and 'romantic' clashed horribly in the same sentence.

'I doubt he'll be able to go, he's so busy. When is it?'

'The last weekend in June.'

'That's in two weeks' time.'

'At our age we can't afford to hang around. Please say you'll come!' She gave a throaty laugh. 'It's not as if you have anything else to do!'

Well, she was right about that.

'OK, I'll come.'

'I'm so pleased. It wouldn't be the same without you!'

Amy hung up and stared into her teacup. Why was it that Eloise's life was always full of adventure? If Amy could have another life, would she marry John? She wasn't so sure any more.

As she expected, John was due to be in Milan the last weekend in June. He didn't mind at all that she go alone, even suggesting she hook up with friends who were also going and make a week of it.

'You deserve a holiday, Amy. It'll do you good to get away.'

So with increasing excitement she bought her plane ticket and packed her bag with summer dresses she usually never got to wear. She had her hair cut and highlighted, and braved a leg wax in anticipation of baring them on those sandy white beaches.

At last, she was on the plane to the Bahamas, from where a smaller plane would take her the short distance to Harbor Island. She left England behind without a single regret and sat back in her seat, sipping Chardonnay and relishing the beginning of what was sure to be a small adventure. It had been years since she had travelled on her own; she felt young again, and free.

As they were about to land at the airport in Nassau, the plane began to judder and jump. Amy gripped the seat. The pilot informed the passengers in his most unflustered voice that they were on the tip of the tail of Hurricane Horace. They'd be lucky to land at all. Amy thought of her children and sent up a quick prayer.

'I promise I'll appreciate my life if you let me live,' she muttered. 'I'll even try to appreciate John.'

Suddenly she longed for his unflappable presence. He was always good in a crisis.

Miraculously, the plane landed safely in Nassau. They were the last flight permitted on to the island. So relieved was she that her prayer had been granted, she didn't mind at all that her connecting flight to Harbor Island was cancelled. She collected her bag and took a taxi to the nearest hotel. Palm trees bent their elegant bodies with nonchalance, and even the taxi driver didn't seem at all concerned that his car might be blown across the road. He'd weathered it all before.

She bathed and dressed, and decided to eat downstairs. After all, she was on holiday. She sat at the bar and ordered a cocktail. There was something delicious about being alone in a strange hotel on the other side of the world, and she found herself laughing out loud.

'What are you laughing at?'

The voice was heavily accented. She turned to see a handsome, dark-haired man sitting alone at the other end of the bar.

'Nothing really,' she replied, taking a sip of her margarita.

'You're lucky you find your own company so amusing,' he said, and she noticed a melancholy shadow in his eyes in spite of his smile.

'I'm on holiday.'

He observed her curiously. 'You might not have noticed, but there's a hurricane outside.'

'Horace. I know. We've already met, thank you.'

He laughed, the shadow lifting as his eyes filled with mirth.

'So, who's the lucky man?'

'What man?' She looked around.

'Are you on your own?'

'Well, you're talking to me, aren't you?'

'Mind if I join you, then? I'm alone too.'

'Have I stumbled into the lonely hearts' club?'

'No, the ante-room before a public hanging.'

She didn't understand his joke, but smiled anyway.

He brought his drink over and sat on the stool beside her.

'What are you having?'

'I was having a margarita.' She lifted her empty glass.

'Can I buy you another? Nothing like a cocktail to make you feel you're on vacation.'

'Are you Italian?'

'Is it that obvious?'

'You're a long way from home.'

'I was sitting there wishing I was home. Then I saw you.'

She looked into his eyes and noticed how engaging

they were. Green like autumn leaves just beginning to turn. He had a sensual face, full lips that curled up at the corners, and a prominent chin with a dimple in the middle.

'You know what that means, don't you?' she said, staring at it.

'What?'

'Well, when you're on the great conveyer belt about to be born, God presses his finger into each belly, like this.'

She gently prodded his shirt.

'You're done, you're done, then, to the very few he puts his thumb here . . .'

She placed hers in the centre of his chin.

'. . . and says softly, "But you're special."'

He laughed. 'I like it.'

'Sweet, isn't it?'

'No, I like the way you touched me.'

She was surprised she didn't blush. 'I'm married.'

'I'm not.'

'Why not?'

'Because no one has ever caught me. I'm a lone wolf.'

She chuckled. 'Maybe you're not worth catching.'

'That's for me to know and for you to find out.'

'You're a terrible flirt.'

'So are you.'

'There's a hurricane outside. We might not make it through the night. Tonight might be our last.'

'If it was our last, what would you do with it?'

She narrowed her eyes, appraising his broad shoulders, open-neck shirt, brown skin and those deeply drawn laughter lines fanning across his temples.

'I wouldn't waste it,' she replied softly, feeling young and brave and reckless.

They dined together, then made their way up to Amy's room. She felt light-headed with alcohol and excitement. Far away from home, she was also far away from herself.

They fell into the room and on to each other. Pinning her against the wall, he buried his face in her neck, tasting the scent of orange blossom on her skin. She closed her eyes and gave way to the sensation of tiny butterfly wings in her belly, so long forgotten that it might as well have been another lifetime. He unzipped her dress and she allowed it to fall into a pool of cotton at her feet. She stood in her panties and bra, head thrown back, aware only of his tongue on her collar bone and his hands on her waist, slowly travelling up towards her breasts.

What happened next was the ride of her life. He made love to her with the patience and the skill Italian men are famous for, and she was swept away on her senses to a place where she was beautiful and valued, with the abandon of a woman who loves only for pleasure.

In the morning he was gone. She lay in the bright sunlight that tumbled in through the window and smiled at the recollection. She didn't feel guilty. After all, she would never see him again. He had been a beautiful stranger who had stepped into her life to remind her that she was still desirable.

Hurricane Horace had moved on, leaving the sky a cerulean blue.

She boarded the little plane in a daze of post-coital bliss. Everything was exquisite, from the crying baby in the front row to the feathery clouds that wafted beneath the plane. The sea sparkled below, and from her heavenly vantage point she knew that her life would never be the same, because she would never again take it for granted. Life was what she made of it.

Eloise looked ravishing in a demure white dress, walking up the beach towards her prince. Then Amy spotted him. It couldn't be. He couldn't have. But he was and he had. It was the Italian from the night before, standing before the vicar, poised to marry her old friend, Eloise.

She felt the blood rush to her face to burn her cheeks with shame and panic.

Before he spotted her she had to have a plan. She thought quickly. Finding a bedroom in the luxurious villa, she hastily cut her hair into a fringe, painted her lips scarlet and covered her lashes in thick mascara. Eloise didn't notice the difference but Riccardo, her husband, blanched at the sight of her.

When Eloise was out of earshot he hissed at her, 'Last night never happened.'

'What are you talking about?'

'In Nassau.'

'I wasn't in Nassau.'

'You weren't?' He looked confused.

'No. I've been here for a few days, but my twin sister Abigail was stuck in some hotel last night due to Hurricane Horace.'

'Your twin sister?' He looked incredulous.

'Yes. It must have been her you met.'

'Perhaps.'

He studied her features, searching for the woman he had made love to the night before. But she did look different.

'We had a drink at the bar, that's all.'

'Great. I'm meeting her tonight. We're booked in for a week at the One & Only.'

'Right.'

'Congratulations, by the way. I hope you make Eloise very happy.'

He watched in bewilderment as she walked away. He didn't notice her legs shaking beneath her sundress.

'She's really lost her looks,' said Eloise when Riccardo caught up with her. 'Big mistake, cutting her fringe like that.'

'I agree. Her sister is much prettier.'

Eloise frowned. 'Sister?'

'I met her in Nassau last night. We had a drink.'

'Honey, she doesn't have a sister.'

He felt the ground fall away beneath him.

'A twin . . .'

His gaze found her in the crowd and he shook his

head at his foolishness. The lone wolf had just got caught, he thought to himself, then he turned sheepishly back to his wife.

Radio Waves

BY JANE MOORE

'*A* fond good morning to all our listeners. It's ten o'clock on a beautifully sunny Saturday morning and we're with you for the next three hours, so sit back and enjoy today's selection of classic summer tunes . . .'

The DJ's voice gives way to the opening bars of the Style Council's 'Long Hot Summer' as I munch disconsolately on a mouthful of dull muesli and stare out of the window. I hate this song. Well, actually, I love it, but I hate the feelings it evokes in me.

I turn to look at Dean, but he's oblivious to the loaded lyrics, chomping on his delicious-smelling bacon sandwich as if it's the Last Supper. He's poring over the new releases in *Computer Games Monthly* magazine, as if he doesn't fritter away enough of his spare time already in front of a small screen.

I think back fondly to the early days, not long after we'd met, when we spent many a wonderful afternoon idling in the sunshine on a pub lawn somewhere, me in a little floral number and 'natural' make-up, still making an effort to look nice for him. These days, it's a denim skirt, vest-top and, mood and time permitting, a smidgen of mascara.

Summer is such a seductive, quixotic time when you're in love and full of dreams, marvelling at the sights and sounds around you as if it's the first time you've seen them. Now it seems like any other time of the year to me, just a bit sweatier.

Two weeks ago, I had enjoyed a holiday to Tenerife with my best friends Saira and Ella and, during the train journey back home from Gatwick airport, I had convinced myself that I'd missed Dean. In my head, at least, he was going to hear my key in the lock and be waiting in the hallway, brimming with affection and tales of how it felt as if I'd been gone for months. Then he'd carry my bags inside, telling me that he'd already planned and bought supper, before carrying me up to bed for wild sex.

Well, my key went in the lock, so that bit happened. But the hallway was empty and, when I called out, a muffled 'Hiya' came back from the living room where, shock horror, the TV wasn't on. But he was stretched out on the sofa, clearly having just woken up.

'What time is it?' he yawned.

'Nine. Two hours since my flight landed,' I replied pointedly.

'Oh, yes.' He stood up and gave me a swift peck on the cheek. 'How was it?'

'Well, we didn't spiral out of the sky and plummet to our deaths, if that's what you mean.'

I had gone through to the bedroom on the pretext of

unpacking my suitcase, but instead I'd slumped on the edge of the bed and felt a debilitating crash of disappointment that swelled to raw irritation when I finally sauntered through to the kitchen and saw the mess.

Dirty plates were stacked up in the sink and on the drainer, and the kitchen table was strewn with three empty pizza boxes and an accompanying plate with crust remnants on it. I suppose I should be grateful he bothered to even use a plate, I'd thought mutinously.

'Sorry.' He'd smiled sheepishly when he saw my expression. 'I was going to get it tidied up before you got back, but I fell asleep and time kind of ran away.'

The desire to snap 'I wish I could run away' was overwhelming, but I stifled it, knowing that, as the one returning from holiday, I was hardly in a position to castigate the one who had stayed behind and worked.

Also, I was feeling badly destabilised by having met Tom in Tenerife. Oh, nothing had happened. At least, nothing more than stimulating conversation and one drunken kiss. But I have been thinking about him a lot, each time prompting butterflies in my stomach. I tell myself that this longing feeling can't be trusted, that it has more to do with the circumstances of subterfuge, sun, sea, sand, lie-ins and liberation from the daily drudgery of work. But even so, when I walked back into my reality of an untidy flat and a boyfriend who seemed distinctly underwhelmed to see me, the emotional crash was huge.

Later on, Dean had alluded to the fact he'd missed

me, by saying something along the lines of: 'It's been quiet around here without you,' though it was hard to tell whether it was meant wistfully or not.

So, as homecomings go, it was pretty low on the scale. Or perhaps my expectations are just too high.

A fortnight on, we've fallen back into our old routine of both traipsing off to work during the week, returning exhausted and unwilling to do much except flop – him in his usual place, me invariably in the bath or reading in bed.

Placing our plates in the sink, I go back to staring out of the window. Our neighbours, Mr and Mrs Payne – I have never known their first names – are in their garden already, probably having risen at four. Mr Payne is sanding down their garden bench and his wife is brutalising a rose bush with secateurs.

But what strikes me is that they're talking, and I mean really talking. Not the occasional remark here and there, but a full-on conversation. I can't hear it, but can tell it's animated by the way she keeps stopping the trimming in order to gesticulate in her husband's direction. He, in turn, smiles at her, then rests his elbows on the back of the bench and adds his two penn'orth. They look so comfortable with one another, yet clearly so interested too. Mrs Payne once told me they'd been together for thirty-five years.

Was there really anything left to say that hadn't already been uttered a hundred times over? In their case, obviously.

Turning back to Dean, I feel a surge of loneliness, a

pang for the life I can see out of my kitchen window, but can't seem to touch myself. On the few occasions that I try to engage Dean in scintillating conversation or even a vaguely interesting one, he nods and grunts in all the right places, but rarely offers an opinion of his own unless there's a tenuous link to sport or mobile phone technology. Perhaps he finds me boring and simply can't be bothered to engage.

It's often said that a successful relationship means leaving three or four things a day unsaid, but in our case most things are unuttered.

I'm not an intellectual heavyweight, or even close, but as I get older I find myself becoming more interested in what's happening in the world around me, yet sharing a home with someone whose interest in anything beyond his own life appears to be diminishing daily. Sometimes, if I stand close enough to him, I swear I can hear the ocean.

We used to have heated debates about everything from politics (he's firmly left wing; I veer to the right) through to whether Bounty or Snickers deserves the title of 'best chocolate bar'. But maybe we've now said all there is to say, and every time a supposedly new subject arises, we both feel we've been there before in some form or other, so there's no fresh perspective to take. So we say little or nothing.

On the radio, someone called Rita tells someone called Alan that she loves him just as much now as she did twenty years ago, and a young man called Alfie tells his girlfriend Julia that, even though it's very early days, he already knows that she's the one. I wish I shared his optimism.

'Now for today's "Where are they now?" appeal,' says the DJ. 'It's not a love story yet, but with our help it just might be . . .'

Waiting for the kettle to boil, I put my mind to what Dean and I can do today. Perhaps a walk along the river and a pub lunch?

'OK, so someone called Tom has written in to the show. He came back from holiday in Tenerife a couple of weeks ago and wants to trace a lovely woman he met there . . .'

My entire body stiffens with tension. Tom . . . Tenerife . . . Two weeks ago . . . It couldn't be, could it? After all, there are thousands of Toms in the country and Tenerife is a big place that thousands fly into every day.

I slowly look back over my shoulder and see Dean still seemingly engrossed in his magazine.

The radio is just a few feet away. I could just nonchalantly walk over and switch it off, just in case . . .

'The woman's name is Cam, short for Camomile, he says . . .'

Too late. The truth is out there, but my fingers are now on the off switch and I'm praying that Dean hasn't heard . . .

'Leave it.' His voice is loud and firm.

My fingers recoil involuntarily. I feel nauseous.

'He just said your name,' says Dean challengingly.

I turn towards him, trying to look puzzled, but the heat burning my face tells me that it's probably give-away pink. My only hope is that he wasn't tuned in to the preamble about 'lovely woman', etc.

I frown, I hope convincingly.

'Yes, I thought that too. But I didn't hear the first bit to know what it was about,' I hedge.

'I did.' He's staring at me intently. 'It's someone called Tom who was in Tenerife two weeks ago, look-ing for a – and I quote – "lovely woman" called Cam, short for Camomile.' His tone is flat. 'Apparently, it's not a love story yet but, and I quote again, "with our help, it just might be".'

'Oh.'

I step backwards and lean against the work surface, unsure what to do or say next. It appears that Dean is quite the multitasker after all, reading a magazine and absorbing every last word of a radio announcement at the same time. Damn.

'As coincidences go, it would be unprecedented.' His mouth sets in a firm line.

He's right, of course. Complete denial would be absolutely futile, but I swiftly assess the situation and decide that I don't have to admit everything.

'OK,' I sigh. 'It is me. But it's nothing, honestly. He's some bloke I met on the first night in a bar, we chatted for a bit, which is why he knows my name . . . Then he flew home very early the next day. It's no big deal.'

'Well, clearly it was to him. You don't go to the

extreme measure of contacting a radio station to find a woman you just chatted to,' he replies contemptuously.

'What are you suggesting?' I fish in desperation.

'I'm not suggesting anything. I'm stating categorically that it stinks.'

We fall silent, him glaring at me, me staring impassively back before finding it uncomfortable and staring down at the floor. I feel both cornered and duplicitous, not a pleasant combination.

It had been a kiss, that's all. If I tried hard enough, I could almost pretend it had never happened, but here it is again, confronting me in the supposed sanctuary of my own kitchen, and in front of the man I have shared so many years with.

'Look, I know it seems an odd thing to do, but I can't be held responsible for the actions of some nutter I met for about five minutes in a bar,' I say eventually. 'I don't mind admitting, I'm as spooked by what we've just heard as you are.'

'Why didn't you tell him you had a boyfriend?'

I shrug. 'The conversation was so fleeting that we barely spoke about anything . . .' Liar, liar. I pause as if trying to remember. 'It was just a bit about the weather and what the hotel was like. The usual polite stuff.'

'So you were staying in the same hotel?' he asks, his eyes narrowing with suspicion.

Oh God, I'm digging myself such a hole here. I feel my face burning and can only hope that, outwardly, it looks normal.

'Yes. It was the hotel bar we met in. Quick chat,

then gone.' I make a slicing gesture across my throat to accentuate the point.

'But long enough for you to tell him your full name, which you normally keep well under your hat,' he says accusingly. 'It took about six months for you to tell me what it was.'

Attack, some say, is the best form of defence. Whatever, right now it feels like my only option. My overwhelming urge is one of protection, to shield Dean from the ugly truth. The power of it takes me by surprise, suggesting as it does that my feelings for him are not as endangered as I have been telling myself.

'Look, Dean . . .' I feign a sigh. 'Please feel free to doubt me, but I'm telling you that nothing happened and if you don't believe me, then I think that speaks volumes about our relationship, don't you?'

Christ, I feel like such a heel. And a cheap one at that. Lying effortlessly has never been my forte, and when it's over something I feel so inexorably guilty and cheap about, it seems infinitely harder.

He doesn't speak, but carries on staring at me impassively for a few seconds, clearly mulling things over. Eventually, he lets out a long sigh.

'OK, fair enough. If you say you only talked to him, then I'll take your word for it. But you really should be more careful in future. He sounds like a potential stalker.'

'I know!' I exclaim, jerking my head towards the radio. 'I was as surprised as you were when I heard that. It didn't even cross my mind that it was anything to do with me until I actually heard my name being read out. I mean, the notion that you'd put out a message for someone you met for a few minutes is insane.'

I realise I am now over-egging it and resist the urge to go on.

Dean stands up and stretches his arms above his head. 'Right. I'm just going to get dressed, then we'll do whatever you've got planned. OK?'

'Sure!' I smile reassuringly.

His willingness to accept my version of events has flooded me with such relief and gratitude that I'd happily sit and watch the football match with him as our afternoon activity. But, of course, as I'm claiming to have done nothing wrong, I have to be careful to keep my behaviour normal.

'I'll just tidy up here first, so let's aim to leave in, ooh, about half an hour?'

He nods and leaves the room. I wait until I hear him enter the bathroom and close the door, then let out a sigh so deep it feels as if every last breath of air has left my body.

Then I pick up the phone . . .

Extracted from Love is On the Air *by Jane Moore.*

The House on the Hill

BY KATE MOSSE

*I*n the house on the hill, there was a light. A single, flickering flame in a room on the first floor. Like a candle burning. Daphne wondered who lived there and resolved to ask her host, Teddy, if it belonged to the Hall.

She stood with her hands on the cold stone window-sill of her bedroom in Dean Hall. In the fading October light, spread out below her lay the fields, furrowed and brown, the glint of white chalk in the soil glistening in the moonlight like fragments of bone.

She shivered, feeling the chill dusk creep over her skin, and withdrew back into her room. She pulled at the window, stiff in its mullioned hinges, and rattled the metal catch until it was properly closed. But she lingered at the window a moment longer, her gaze fixed upon the speck of light on the distant hills, until suddenly it was gone. If she'd been a jumpy kind of a girl, she might have gasped. As it was, Daphne felt rather put out, as if she had been snubbed or been caught snooping.

She thought of her temporary room in the boarding

house in Berwick Street, the single gas ring in the kitchen shared by four girls like her, who had not been brought up to earn a living by typing or working in a shop. She thought of the tatty WC at the end of the corridor, the nylon stockings hanging over the bath, the scarcity of hot water, and could have cried for the world she found herself in. If Douglas had not run out on her, life would have been so different. Mrs Daphne Dumsilde. It had such a ring to it. Douglas had promised to look after her, in sickness and in health. But he had not.

Daphne shook her head, irritated at how easily she had allowed herself to slip back into her habitual gloomy state of mind. Why spoil a perfectly pleasant weekend? Invitations had been thin on the ground – a woman alone was always awkward and her circumstances made it doubly so. Here there would be plenty of hot water, plenty of food and drink, perhaps a little dancing and amusing company to keep the dark thoughts at bay. She should enjoy herself. Appreciate being out of London.

She walked to the dresser and took a cigarette from her case. She tapped it sharply to tighten the tobacco, picked up her Ronson and jabbed at it with her thumb until it sparked. That, too, reminded her of Douglas.

Daphne inhaled, feeling the calming smoke trickle down into her lungs. Her jumping heart steadied. From the oak hall below, she heard the sound of the gramophone and whispers of jazz. Oddly modern music for so antique a setting. She glanced back to the window, her eye drawn by the echo of the light on the hill, but dusk had fallen, stripping the shape and character from the pleasant Sussex landscape.

Daphne stubbed out her cigarette and quickly dressed for dinner. She hesitated a moment, then removed her wedding ring and left it on the table beside the bed.

Her bedroom was in the south wing, which meant she had to walk past the doll's house on the long corridor on her way down. There were ribbons of dust on the slope of its red-tiled roof and tall chimneys, but it was beautiful still. Tonight there appeared to be a fire burning in a grate of one of the tiny bedrooms. Daphne knew it must be some kind of clever electric trick, but it looked so real she could not resist opening up the front to investigate.

The white wooden façade swung back, revealing the entire household within from top to bottom. Daphne cast her eyes over each of the rooms in turn, but could not work out where the light had been. There were lamp fittings on the balsa-wood walls, but they didn't work.

She glanced over her shoulder, wondering if perhaps the electric light in the corridor might somehow have bounced off the glass front of the display cabinet and given the impression of something shining inside the doll's house. Straightaway, she saw that was impossible. The angle was all wrong. Daphne shivered, disliking the hard black eyes and frozen feathers of the robins, blackbirds and cranes motionless behind the glass.

The evening passed in a haze of vermouth and ragtime and pheasant, all pleasant enough, blotting out the memory of the drab life to which she would have to return on Monday morning. The company was congenial and she flirted a little with a boy who worked in a dispensary. While the men talked finance, Daphne talked about the latest detective novels to a girl from Surrey, some vague relation of Teddy's. With an intimacy established, she could see the girl was on the point of asking about Douglas. Daphne excused herself and went in search of coffee. It was, Daphne thought savagely, why she rarely ventured out in society. It was dull always to have all eyes on her, wondering and thinking.

Her room was cold and the maid had not closed the curtains. As she climbed into bed, she told herself the evening had been a welcome change from scratch suppers eaten alone with only a paperback book for company, but she couldn't pretend she felt less lonely than usual.

Looking back, Daphne never worked out what it was that woke her. One moment she was fast asleep, dreaming. The next, she was wide awake, heart pounding. The silence of the sleeping house surged around her, punctuated by the gurgling of the water pipes.

But yet there was something. As if the air itself was alive, brittle and sharp.

Daphne waited for her eyes to adjust. Then, she saw

it. Through the window, in the same place as before, a flickering light in the house up on the hill, flames flickering and dancing. Except this time they were fiercer, more insistent, certainly not a single candle.

She sat bolt upright in her bed. The house on the hill was burning.

Daphne flung back the covers and jumped out of bed, banging her shin on its wooden corner. She pushed her feet into her walking boots, put her hat on her head and her coat over the top of her pyjamas, and ran down the corridor, raising the alarm. She hurtled down the main stairs, unbolted the heavy front door and flew out into the night. Somehow, she should help. The others would follow. They would see what she had seen, and follow.

Daphne ran across the lawns and up into the pastures above the Hall. Her breath burned ragged in her throat and the muscles complained in her thighs and calves, but she kept going. Grey clouds scudded across the face of the moon, sending slats of silver shadows like streamers over the grass.

Then Daphne caught a glimpse of someone else on the hillside, ahead of her, also heading towards the house.

'Wait!' she cried out, but the man did not falter. He did not even turn around.

Daphne kept going, taking long strides, half stumbling, half running, keeping him in her sights. The closer she got, the more she felt there was something familiar. The cut of his jacket, his profile in the flat white light.

Suddenly, between the trees, there was the house itself. She stopped dead. It was just as she had imagined it would be. Perfectly beautiful, a white, wooden, painted façade, sloping, red-tiled roof and tall stack chimneys. In fact, the original of the doll's house on the first floor of the Hall.

There was no sign of the man. What was more, Daphne realised there was no crackling of flames, no heat, no sign that anything was wrong. There was only a single flame, like a candle, that she had noticed earlier in the same first-floor room. The same place where she had seen a pinprick of light in the doll's house. A trickle of cold ran like a finger down her spine.

Daphne saw the front door was open. She took a step towards it, hesitated, then another step. Had the man already gone in?

'Is anyone here?'

No one answered. She walked into the house, across the red-and black-tiled entrance hall, and up the stairs. Now she could hear the ticking of the clock, and the crack, spit and roar of an open fire. Where was everybody?

Looking back, Daphne thought it queer that it did not even occur to her to leave. Something was drawing her towards that bedroom on the first floor. At the top of the stairs, she turned right. The door at the end of the corridor was ajar. One step further, and another. Now she was pushing it slowly open.

Inside, she found a plain bedroom, a pretty counterpane, a tortoiseshell picture frame on the nightstand beside the bed and a single candle burning. Daphne went towards it and held her hand to the flame, then quickly withdrew it.

Her heart tripped a beat. She could feel there was someone in the room with her.

Slowly, she turned. And saw the image that, for five years, had haunted her dreams. Slowly, she raised her eyes. And saw feet swinging in the air, legs, dangling hands, the body. A man hanging, twisting in the still air.

'No,' she murmured, 'no.'

She made herself look at the man's face, knowing what she would see.

Douglas, just as she had found him dead in his parents' house five years ago. Douglas, who had promised to look after her, in sickness and in health, but who had left her. Unable to live with his memories of gas and barbed wire and his friends dying in the mud of Flanders and France, he had left her to cope alone.

Daphne screamed.

They found her hours later, lying on the open hillside above the Hall. The warm October light had already painted the world in vivid colours: yellow and orange and magenta. The leaves on the oak trees were shimmering silver in the light breeze.

She was lucky, they said. A small fire had broken out in an airing cupboard in the south wing, just below Daphne's bedroom, and quickly spread. The old summer curtains and brocade stored on the wooden slatted shelves had burned like paper. She wouldn't have stood a chance. She would have been overcome by smoke long before the fire had reached her.

No one else had been in danger, though the house had been evacuated. Her bedroom and several others, all unoccupied, had been damaged, and the old doll's house on the landing had been badly burned, though it was some way from the heart of the fire.

It was only as dawn broke and everyone trooped back into the house that they realised Daphne wasn't there. She wasn't in her room, but when they'd scoured the house from top to bottom and still not found her, they started to fear the worst. It was only when Teddy remembered Daphne asking questions about the estate that they thought to search the park itself. One of the outside servants went up the hill towards the woods and found her, unconscious on the ground, and brought her back.

Daphne tried to explain how she had seen a light burning in the house on the hill, about the man who had led her away from the Hall. About Douglas.

They didn't understand. There was no other house on the estate, they told her. And everyone else was accounted for. No one else had left the Hall. And, though they smiled and patted her hand, she could see they thought she was in shock. That she was imagining things. And the pity in their eyes burned her and she fell silent and turned away.

But later, when Daphne lay back on the soft pillows,

having accepted Teddy's invitation to stay at Dean Hall until she felt well enough to go back to London, she began to plan. How she would leave Berwick Street and return to the little house in Chelsea she had abandoned after Douglas's death. How she would start again.

Douglas had promised to look after her. In the end, he had. He had saved her, though he had not been able to save himself. Now she could begin to forgive him for leaving her. Grieve for him, miss him, but move forward. Now, it was up to her. Next year would be better. It was time to begin again.

Crocodile Shoes

BY JOJO MOYES

She is peeling her way out of her wet costume when the Yummy Mummies arrive. Glossy and stick thin, they surround her, talking loudly, completely oblivious to her presence.

These are women with designer gymwear, perfect hair and time for coffee. She imagines husbands called Rupe or Tris who carelessly toss envelopes containing awesome bonuses onto their Conran kitchen tables. These women do not have husbands who stay in their pyjama bottoms till midday and look hunted whenever their wives mention having another go at that job application.

Gym membership is a luxury they really cannot afford these days, but Sam is tied into paying for it for another four months and Phil tells her she might as well make the most of it. It does her good, he says. He means: to get out of the house and away from him.

'Use it or lose it, Mum,' says their daughter, who eyes Sam's increasingly indistinct hip-to-waist ratio with barely concealed horror. She cannot tell either of them how much she hates the gym: its apartheid of hard bodies, the corners where she and the other Lumpy People try to hide.

She is at that age, the age where all the wrong things seem somehow to stick – fat, the groove between her eyebrows – while everything else – job security, marital happiness, dreams – seem to slip effortlessly away.

'You have no idea how much they've put up the prices at Club Med this year,' one of the women is saying. She is bent over, towelling her expensively tinted hair. Sam has to wiggle sideways to avoid touching her.

'I know! I tried to book Mauritius for Christmas – our usual villa has gone up by forty per cent.'

'It's a scandal.'

Yes, it's a scandal, she thinks. How awful for you all. She thinks of the caravan that Phil bought the previous year to do up. We can spend weekends by the coast, he had said, cheerfully. He never got beyond repairing the back bumper. Since he lost his job, it has sat there on the drive, a nagging reminder of what they had lost.

Sam wriggles into her knickers, trying to hide her pale flesh under the towel. Today she has four meetings with potential clients. In half an hour she will meet Ted and Joel from Print, and they will try to win their company some vital business. No pressure there, then.

'Do you remember that awful place in Cannes that Susanna booked?'

They are braying with laughter. Sam pulls her towel

more tightly around her and disappears around the corner to dry her hair.

When she returns they are gone. She breathes a sigh of relief and slumps down on the damp wooden bench.

It is only when she is dressed that she reaches under the bench and realises that although the kitbag there looks exactly like hers, it is not hers. This bag does not contain her comfortable black pumps, suitable for pounding pavements and negotiating deals. It contains a pair of vertiginous, red, crocodile-skin, Christian Louboutin sling-backs.

The woman at the desk doesn't blink.

'The girl who was in the changing rooms. She's taken my bag.'

'What's her name?'

'I don't know. There were three of them. One of them took my bag.'

'Sorry, but I usually work at the Hills Road branch. You're probably best off speaking to someone who works here full time.'

'But I have meetings to go to now. I can hardly go in my trainers.'

The way the girl stares at her suggests that wearing trainers is the least of Sam's sartorial worries. She glances at her phone. She is due at the first meeting in thirty minutes. She sighs, picks up the kitbag and stomps off towards the train.

*

She cannot go into this meeting in gym shoes. This becomes obvious as soon as she reaches the publishers, whose plush marble and gilt offices make Trump Towers look restrained. It is also apparent in Ted and Joel's sideways glances at her feet.

'Getting down with the yoof, are we?' Joel says.

'Going to wear your leotard too?' says Ted.

She hesitates, then curses, rummages around in the bag and pulls out the shoes. They are only half a size out. Without saying anything, she whips off her trainers in the foyer and puts on the red Louboutins instead. When she stands, she has to grab Joel's arm to stay upright.

'Wow. They're um . . . not very you.'

She straightens, glares at Joel. 'Why, what's "me"?'

'Plain. You like plain stuff. Sensible stuff.'

Ted smirks. 'You know what they say about shoes like that, Sam.'

'What?'

'Well, they're not for standing up in.'

They nudge each other, chuckling. Great, she thinks. So I get to go to a meeting looking like a call-girl.

When she emerges from the lift, it is all she can do to walk across the room. She feels stupid, as if everyone is looking at her, as if it is obvious that she is a middle-aged woman in somebody else's shoes. She stammers her way through the meeting and stumbles as she leaves. The two men say nothing, but they all know that they will not get this contract. Nevertheless, she has no choice. She will have to wear the ridiculous shoes all day.

'Never mind. Still three to go,' says Ted, kindly.

She is outlining their print strategy in the second meeting when she observes that the managing director is not listening to her. He is staring at her foot. Embarrassed, she almost loses the thread of what she is saying. But then she realises it is he who is distracted.

'So how do those figures sound?' she says.

'Good!' he exclaims, as if hauled from a daydream. 'Yes. Good.'

She senses a brief opportunity, pulls a contract from her briefcase. 'So, shall we agree terms?'

He is staring at her shoes again. She tilts one foot and lets the strap slide from her heel.

'Sure,' he says. He takes the pen without looking at it.

'Don't say anything,' she says to Ted, as they leave, jubilant.

'I'm saying nothing. You get us another deal like that, you can wear carpet slippers for all I care.'

At the next meeting she makes sure her feet are on display the whole time. Although John Edgmont doesn't stare, she sees that the mere fact of these shoes makes him reassess his version of who she is. Weirdly, it makes her reassess her version of herself. She charms. She stands firm on terms. She wins another contract.

They take a taxi to meeting four.

'I don't care,' she says. 'I can't walk in these things, and I've earned it.'

The result is that instead of their usual harried, sweaty arrival, she pulls up outside the final meeting unruffled. She steps out and realises that she is standing taller.

She is a little disappointed therefore to discover M. Price is a woman. And it doesn't take long to discover that Miriam Price plays hardball. The negotiations take an hour. If they go ahead their margins will be down to almost nothing. It feels impossible.

'I just need to visit the ladies' room,' Sam says. Once inside, she stares at herself in the mirror, wondering what to do.

The door opens and Miriam Price steps in behind her. They nod politely while washing their hands. And then Miriam Price looks down.

'Oh my God, I love your shoes,' she exclaims.

'Actually they're—' Sam begins. Then she stops. 'They're great, aren't they?'

Miriam points down at them. 'Can I see?'

She holds the shoe that Sam removes, examines it from all angles.

'Is this a Louboutin?'

'Yes.'

'You know I once queued for four hours just to buy a pair of his shoes. How crazy is that?'

'Oh, not crazy at all,' says Sam.

Miriam Price hands it back almost reluctantly. 'You know, you can always tell a proper shoe. My daughter doesn't believe me, but you can tell so much about someone from what they wear.'

'I tell my daughter the exact same thing!' The words are out of her mouth before she even knows what she's saying.

'I tell you what. I hate negotiating like this. Do you have a window for lunch next week? Let's the two of us get together and thrash something out.'

'That would be great,' Sam says. She manages to walk out of the Ladies without the slightest wobble.

She arrives home after seven. She is in her trainers again and her daughter, who is just headed out, raises her eyebrows as if she is some kind of bag lady.

'This is not New York, Mum. You just look weird, like you lost your shoes.'

'I did lose my shoes.' She puts her head around the living-room door. 'Hey.'

'Hey!'

Phil raises a hand. He is where she knew he'd be: on the sofa. 'Have you . . . done anything about supper?'

'Oh. No. Sorry.'

It's not that he is selfish. It's as if he cannot rouse himself to anything any more, even the cooking of beans on toast. The successes of the day evaporate. She makes supper, and then as an afterthought pours two glasses of wine.

'You'll never guess what happened to me today,' she says, handing one to him. And she tells him the story of the swapped shoes.

'Show me.'

She heads out into the hallway and puts them on. She straightens a little as she walks back into the living room, injects a little swagger into her walk.

'Wow.'

'I know! I wouldn't have bought them in a million years. And they're a nightmare to walk in. But I pulled in three deals today, three deals we weren't expected to get. And I think it was all because of the shoes.'

'Not all of it, surely. But your legs look fantastic.'

She smiles. 'Thank you.'

'You never wear shoes like this.'

'I know. I don't have a Louboutin shoe sort of life.'

'You should. You look . . . you look amazing.'

He looks so lovely then, so pleased for her and yet so vulnerable. She walks over to her husband, sits on his lap, links her arms around his neck. Perhaps the wine has made her giddy. She cannot remember the last time she approached him like this. They gaze at each other.

'You know what they say about shoes like this?' she murmurs.

He blinks.

'Well, they're not made for standing up in.'

She is at the gym shortly after nine on Saturday morning. She is not here to thrash up and down the pool, or strap herself to one of their merciless machines. She has a different ache, one that makes her blush faintly with pleasure. She has come to return the shoes.

She pauses in front of the glass doors, remembering Phil's face as he woke her with a mug of coffee.

'I thought I'd start on that caravan today,' he said, cheerfully. 'Might as well make myself useful.'

It is then that she sees the woman at the reception desk. It is one of the Yummy Mummies, her hair in a glossy ponytail, railing at one of the staff. On the desk is a familiar kitbag. She hesitates, feeling a reflexive clench of inadequacy.

Sam looks down at the bag by her feet. She will not come to this gym again. She suddenly knows this as surely as she knows anything. She will not be swimming, or sweating, or hiding in corners. She takes a breath, strides in and puts the bag down in front of the woman.

'You know, you really should check that you pick up the right bag,' she says, as she grabs her own. 'Taking someone else's shoes? It's a scandal.'

Sam turns on her heel. She is still laughing when she reaches the train station. She has a bonus payment that is burning a hole in her pocket. And a pair of very unsuitable shoes to purchase.

Quality Time

BY FIONA NEILL

*I*t was Tom's idea to come here. Hayley had favoured a long weekend in Rome. But Tom had argued with unusual vehemence that, on the eve of their fifteenth wedding anniversary, they should revisit the country where they had fallen in love. The children, now in their early teens, could spend half-term with friends. It was the right moment, he insisted, to rediscover the spirit of adventure that had brought them together in the first place.

'Let's live a little,' he'd said, reaching out to touch her forearm, 'get out of our comfort zone. And no cheap hotels this time, I promise.'

Besides, they already had the guidebook. He had duly presented her with their tatty old copy of *The Rough Guide to Tunisia*, published in the early 1990s. As he pressed it into her hands Hayley had instinctively lifted the book to her nose. It smelled hot and sweet, and fell open on a chapter headed 'Tozeur and the Jerid'. Something fell from the page: a dried oleander bloom that Tom had picked for her during their trip almost two decades earlier. The children groaned as they always did when they sensed a rare moment of sentimentality between their parents. And Hayley capitulated, unable to resist the nostalgia of his notion.

'Great,' she said swiftly, aware that if she thought about it too long, she might find reasons not to go.

'Really?' he had responded.

'Really,' she had reiterated, gratified she could still surprise him.

And so, instead of resting a cheek against a cool marble pillar in the Sistine Chapel to stare up at Eve emerging from Adam's side, Hayley now found herself squinting at the biscuit-coloured minaret of a mosque just outside Tozeur, trying to remember how she felt when she saw it for the first time all those years ago.

'We used to be so free,' she said wistfully, craning to look at the top of the tower, admiring the exotic geometric patterns and wondering who came to worship in this apparently deserted village on the road towards Algeria. She felt Tom touch her neck and leaned towards him. He kissed her quickly on the lips.

Hayley wiped her forehead again. Hotter. She definitely felt hotter than she could ever remember. Her eyes were half closed against the sun and the sky, which had turned from blue to orange in the time they had been standing here. As she licked beads of sweat from her upper lip, she could feel that already, less than half an hour after leaving the air-conditioned sanctuary of their boutique hotel, she was already baked inside a shroud of dust. They had come at the same time of year as their last visit. So was the impossible heat due to global warming or peri-menopause, she wondered?

'Water?' She took a long swig from her bottle and passed it to Tom. It was already warm. He shook his head.

'Go easy on the liquid,' he said, 'it just makes you sweat more.'

'We've got two gallons in the back of the car,' she said, but her words were carried away by the wind, which seemed stronger away from the oasis of Tozeur.

Tom ignored her and continued reading from the guidebook. She tried to concentrate on what he was saying but was distracted by the sight of an elderly Bedouin man loping towards them on a mule. He stopped almost beside them and stared, his hand resting protectively on a large sack.

'We don't want any carpets,' said Tom abruptly, without looking up from the book, as the man opened up the bag.

'As-salaam alaykum,' said Hayley, pleased her memory hadn't betrayed her.

She pulled a scarf around her head, less out of any sense of propriety than the urge to keep the dust out of her hair and the heat off her head. When they had arrived yesterday, she had laughed at the tourists trying to pass themselves off as nomads by wearing blue scarves wrapped around their faces and necks. Now she was one of them.

'They don't say that in Tunisia,' Tom murmured.

Hayley noticed that the small bald patch on the top

of his head was looking red even though the rest of his face was already turning steadily browner.

'Haboob.' The man smiled, pointing at the sky. 'Haboob.'

'Don't engage or he'll try to sell you something,' Tom reminded her. 'We don't have much time.'

Hayley winced. Last time they were here, Tom and she had spent hours sharing tea and *shisha* with villagers. At the time she thought it was an appealing part of her new boyfriend's personality. Now she realised it probably had more to do with the fact that he was working on a documentary series on nomads of the Maghreb.

She recalled the sense of hope and optimism of that first trip. She had known Tom less than three months when he had suggested she fly to meet him at the end of his work trip. She was twenty-three and had just finished an MA in English Literature. He was already working in the documentaries department at the BBC. Her elder brother had introduced them with a warning that Tom wasn't 'good relationship material'. She had ignored him and bought a ticket to Tunis. Within three years they were married and a couple of years later Gus was born, hastily followed by Felix.

Hayley wanted to tell him that he needed to slow down. That it didn't matter if they didn't make it to the desert today, that the Dar Charait museum could wait until tomorrow. They could go back to Tozeur, spend the afternoon in bed and then walk round the welcome cool of the oasis in the evening if they wanted. They could even spend the whole day in bed. When was the last time they had done that?

Hayley still travelled with hope. Now aged forty-three, her aspirations were less epic and more specific than they had been two decades ago, and mostly involved her children because she was no longer sure what she wanted herself.

She closed her eyes again and breathed in the rich smell of aniseed as the man opened up his sack.

'It's fennel,' she exclaimed triumphantly.

The man pressed a bulb into her hand, looking pleased with her reaction. He pointed at the sky. 'Haboob,' he repeated several times before climbing back on his mule.

'Thank you,' shouted Hayley after him.

'It was built in the ninth century and the raised brickwork laid in contrary directions is unique to this region of Tunisia,' said Tom, reading from the guide-book.

'Mmm,' said Hayley.

The wind blew a new wave of sand and dust across the road and over Hayley. Ashes to ashes, dust to dust, she thought to herself. The desert could consume a body as fast as any hyena.

'What do you think?' Tom asked, in the way he might once have questioned the children when reading a bedtime story to check they were concentrating.

'I think it looks like a piece of giant shortbread,' replied Hayley with satisfaction, assuming he was asking her opinion about the mosque.

'You're not listening to me,' said Tom, heading back towards the car. 'I was saying that I think it would be a good idea to hit the dunes before the masses arrive.'

He headed for the car so fast that she found herself caught in a slipstream of dust. As they climbed into the front, Hayley noticed that behind them the sky was turning grey.

'Rain?' Hayley shouted over the noise of the wind.

'According to the guidebook it hasn't rained here for half a century,' said Tom, as he switched on the engine.

They left the village behind them and turned up the radio to listen to gravelly songs in Arabic on a local radio station as they headed west towards the Algerian border, where the rough, flat edges of the Sahara turned into huge, imposing sand dunes.

'Why were you rude to that man?' Hayley suddenly asked, as she stared out of the window, wondering if this really was the same route they had followed twenty years earlier. All the roads in this region looked the same.

Tom apologised and tried to explain that perhaps it wasn't such a great idea to come back to a place that you had been before because it increased the possibilities of nostalgia and regret. His comment stung Hayley.

'What I mean is that the era of mass tourism has reached the Sahara and I don't like the way everything has become so commercialised. Last time we were here there were four land cruisers in Tozeur to take tourists to the dunes and now there are hundreds,' Tom hastily added. 'It's all those *Star Wars* aficionados. God, did you see that American guy in the lobby this morning dressed up as Luke Skywalker? And the women with their Princess Leia plaits?'

Hayley remained silent. She would have liked to visit the old *Star Wars* sets in Matmâta and knew that Tom would probably indulge her if she suggested going there now.

'If you go somewhere you've never been before, then you don't have points of comparison,' Tom continued, anxiously glancing over at her. 'I guess I had too many expectations.'

She stuffed a couple of dates into her mouth in case she was tempted to give in, and chewed them in silence.

'I wasn't talking about us, Hayley,' Tom said finally.

The long silence was filled with the sound of a commentator gabbling in Arabic on the radio. Then a familiar song came on.

'Oasis playing in the oasis,' joked Tom.

'So each time you slept with her did you regret it a little bit more?' Hayley blurted out. Her words hung in the air.

'It was over before it even began, Hayley,' Tom said gently, 'And yes, actually, I did.'

There was another gaping silence.

'Can't we put it behind us? Please. It was meaningless.'

He switched on the wipers to try to clean the dust from the windscreen and Hayley was grateful for the noise as they squeaked back and forth.

'You're the one who always wants to be somewhere

else,' Hayley responded. 'And when I'm with you and you're in that kind of mood, it makes me feel as if you'd rather be with someone else, and that makes me feel that maybe you should be with someone else.'

The words tumbled out of Hayley's mouth before she had any time for self-censorship.

It was an ancient argument. So familiar that it had come to feel like the script of someone else's life. Why had he done it? Why? When they had got through the grind of the early years, when Gus and Felix were almost independent and they were beginning to rediscover life together? Why had he chosen that moment to embark on a casual affair with a researcher at work? It had happened on location, he explained, as though that accounted for what he described as 'his serious lapse of judgement'.

They had unexpectedly come to a fork in the road. Hayley turned the map several times in her lap. Tom switched off the engine. She turned round to look at a sign beside them. 'Attention Passage Dromadaires' it read. Nothing to indicate the road to Nefta.

'Do you know where we are?' Tom asked.

He tentatively wound down the window to look back down the desolate road. Sand blew in and the wind roared as loud as the sea as it rocked the stationary car.

'God, what's going on?' asked Hayley, through the grit between her teeth.

They both turned round to stare out the back windscreen and saw a thick soupy brown cloud behind them.

'Sandstorm,' they both said simultaneously.

Tom swiftly shut the window again. The key strategy in a sandstorm was to stay in exactly the same place because within minutes the road would be covered, he commented, pulling out his BlackBerry from the glove compartment.

He had once been in a sandstorm when he was filming in Morocco, he reassured Hayley. 'Oh – there's no reception.'

He took the map from her lap and tried to identify where they might be.

'It's inaccurate,' said Hayley, opening a couple of guidebooks to compare different versions of the same area. 'They're all different.'

Her teeth were chattering from the sudden drop in temperature.

'We should get the food and water from the boot,' she suggested.

'And our clothes,' said Tom, 'in case we end up spending the night here.'

'You were right. We shouldn't have come,' said Hayley.

'It was my idea.' Tom shrugged.

'But you expected me to say no,' said Hayley.

They smiled tentatively at each other.

The car was enveloped by the cloud of sand and grit. Hayley could no longer see the sign warning about camels on the road, but at least the dust muffled the noise of the wind.

'I wonder whether sandstorms have an eye, like a

hurricane, and if they do, whether we are almost at its apex?' Tom asked.

'Do you think we could get buried?' Hayley responded. 'Is there such a thing as an avalanche of sand? Could we suffocate?'

'We have to fight the urge to get out of the car,' insisted Tom.

He held her hand and they stared out the windscreen as sand fell on the glass like tiny drops of rain.

'In a situation like this, it is critical not to lose your nerve.'

'What would Ray Mears do?' Hayley wondered.

'He would tell us to pee in a container in case we run out of water,' said Tom, picking up an empty plastic bottle from the floor in front of Hayley. Despite herself, she laughed.

'We're not going to die,' said Tom.

'We're not going to die,' Hayley reiterated.

She shivered again and Tom suggested they lie across the back seat to maximise their body heat and cover themselves with spare clothes. Tom offered to go on the outside edge and they lay there staring out the window as the sandstorm enveloped them. Hayley glanced at her watch and told Tom that they shouldn't look again because it would make the time pass more slowly. Tom pulled an iPod from the bag and they each chose songs for one another. He put his arm around her.

'We're good together, Hayley,' he said.

'We are,' she admitted.

'I'm really sorry,' he said.

Then, as quickly as it had descended, the cloud of sand began to disappear. They got out of the car, scarves wrapped around their noses and mouths. It had blown itself out in less than half an hour, but the road was totally obscured.

'What do we do now?' asked Hayley, warily eyeing the desolate, empty landscape.

'We wait,' said Tom. 'The desert is full of tourists.'

They leaned against the car, enjoying the heat of the sun on their skins. Tom read from his guidebook.

'We must be very close to where those Austrian tourists were kidnapped by Al-Qaeda,' Tom suddenly said. 'It says they came across the border from Algeria.'

He put up a hand to shield his eyes. In the distance they could both see the glint of a car windscreen approaching.

'What happened to them?' Hayley asked.

'One was killed, the other released,' said Tom.

The car was travelling fast, its driver utterly assured of his whereabouts, despite the disappearance of the asphalt road. They stood waving their arms in a spot that might have been the middle of the road. As it drew closer the driver slowed down and they could see a group of people in the back wearing scarves around their faces and carrying what looked like guns.

'Shit,' said Hayley.

'Could be Berber tribesmen,' said Tom sounding nervous for the first time. 'It would be really bad luck, after everything that's happened, to end up bumping into a bunch of jihadists in the desert.'

The car pulled up and the door opened. Out got the man they had seen in the hotel that morning. He was carrying a lightsabre.

'God, am I pleased to see you,' said Tom.

'May the force be with you,' joked the man.

Sunny Aspect

BY ELIZABETH NOBLE

*T*he smell of old dog assailed Cassie's nostrils as soon as she let herself in with the keys the owner had left in the office on her way to work. The offending creature was sniffing her suspiciously now, too old and exhausted to jump up in defence of his home. She let him into the garden and shut the french doors firmly behind him, although she opened the two sash windows on either side of the fireplace as wide as she could.

She always liked to arrive a few minutes early. To titivate, as her mother would have called it. Half an hour, for this property, if she could manage it. The lady of the house thought nothing of leaving damp tights and greying bras hanging from the radiators, empty milk cartons on the kitchen work surface, and Lego Armageddon on the sitting-room rug – and that was no way to showcase a house. No way to showcase your life either, but Cassie wasn't here to judge.

What Cassie could, and was, here to do was a near miracle, given thirty minutes, a spray bottle of Febreze and an appraising eye. Everyone in the office said so.

All the new agents were sent out with her in their first week to see how it was done. If it wasn't quite the smell of fresh baked bread and brewing coffee that greeted the prospective buyers when they arrived, it was at least a little less Eau de Fido.

It wasn't about masking problems, it was just about making it easier to see the bones of a place. Easier to imagine yourself living there. That was the trick.

She was getting to know this couple: they'd been looking for a while. Newly-weds. She wanted a home. He wanted a smart investment. The woman liked it. The husband would take some persuading. Cassie always knew, almost straightaway. Women were easier to read, she thought – they gave away more with their polite running commentaries and their body language.

The woman stood at the sink and gazed out of the window to the garden beyond, with its climbing frame and swing set and, for just a moment, she pretended it – all of it – was hers. Cassie could see it. But maybe that was because she was a woman too . . .

Estate agent. It wasn't the career she'd imagined for herself, when she was younger. Her childish imagination had been more fecund than that – it had placed her, at night, as she lay dreaming in her narrow single bed, in infinitely more glamorous situations. A film star or a countess, perhaps. A singing diva, like Barbra Streisand in *Funny Girl*. All nonsensical, whimsical fantasies, of course, as her mother had pointed out.

Truthfully, she probably hadn't pictured a career at

all. There had been a vast difference between her dreams at night and her expectations during daylight hours. A job, perhaps, while she waited for a man to marry her (or was that rescue her?). Then a few children and a home to 'run'. A schooner of sherry on Sunday mornings while she cooked the roast and he played a round at the club.

But it was, after all, a career. A career she loved. Partly it was because she knew she was good at it and, although it wasn't a character trait of which she was particularly proud, she liked things better when she was good at them. It was the reason she never played tennis and her motivation for doing the *Times* crossword daily.

Partly, too, she knew it satisfied what had always been her tremendous curiosity about other people and the way they lived. Her mother had called her Sticky Beak when she was a girl, and insinuated that her nosiness was somehow mean or inappropriate. But she had never believed that herself and at some point in her twenties she'd realised, though not ever fully understood why, that her mother never saw the best in her when she could see the worst. Cassie was interested, that was all. People fascinated her. Everyone had a story, and their best ones weren't told in words.

But mostly, she told herself – as well as anyone who asked her why she did what she did – she thought she liked helping people. Like a doctor or a hairdresser, she could fix problems and facilitate changes, because where you lived was one of the most important things about you. And she played a part in that process. She had done so for hundreds and hundreds of people.

It was only relatively recently, though, that the thought had occurred to her that most of the homes she viewed reflected back at her some image of experiences she herself had had, or might have had, perhaps, if she'd chosen a different path through the maze of her life. It entranced her, that idea.

She imagined herself, now, in every interior she saw. She smiled at the memory of a younger her – twenty, thirty years ago, with a bad haircut, pixie boots and a serious Bruce Springsteen habit – as she measured and photographed the single woman's neat, designer flat. She'd never had anywhere this nice, but she'd had somewhere. She'd known both the liberating joy and the crushing loneliness of living alone. No one to stop you eating a whole cake in front of a weepie. And no one to notice if you stayed all day in your room, crying over someone who'd broken your heart.

This girl – the one with the Cath Kidston oilcloth on the table and the fresh flowers every week – was getting married: a teetering pile of wedding magazines and invitation samples sat boasting smugly on the coffee table. Cassie had never been married.

Nor had she ever been a harassed young mother, like the one selling the house that smelled of dog, too busy and too exhausted by trying to have it all to actually do any of it very well. Perhaps she was supposed to feel envy when she was here, looking at proudly displayed finger-paintings and ironing piles on every chair, but she felt something she thought might just be relief.

And it was hard to envy the inhabitants of the two big houses she had on her list at the top end of town – the posh part where the streets widened and were lined with trees. Gin palaces, her mother would have called them.

One was a bank repossession, its Jacuzzi bathtub and built-in coffee machine mocking the former owner. Things had never mattered that much to Cassie. People mattered. Things were set dressing. It was important only to be comfortable, and comfort was her greatest luxury. The marble and granite and state-of-the-art speakers hadn't brought happiness. And, now, with the place stripped bare, Cassie's voice echoed in the cavernous hallway as she extolled the virtues of the view no one was looking at and the swimming pool no one swam in.

In the other house, smaller, but almost as swanky, with three small cars on the driveway, the husband had left. The wife, still svelte and made-up, but nervous and hollow-eyed, her children grown beyond the point of needing her, looked utterly broken as she showed Cassie around, her arms gesturing loosely at spaces as though she was trying to push memories away.

Cassie didn't know what had gone wrong, though she understood enough after all these years to know there were clichés and stereotypes, and then there was the truth. She'd gone out with men, when she was younger: men who might have been able to provide her with this life, the life she'd been raised to think she should want. And who might have left her, just at that point when she was least able to cope with it.

Her last viewing of the day was the small, tired bungalow near the centre of town. She showed a young man around. He'd watched one too many property shows on the television and had grand plans to renovate and sell at a profit. Great position, he said. Shame about everything else.

Shame about him, Cassie thought. She didn't always care so much about what happened to a home, but she cared about this one. It had belonged to a couple who'd been married for more than sixty-five years. The local newspaper had done an article on them, on their sixtieth anniversary, and it was framed and hung on the wall next to family photographs – their children, their grandchildren, and their great-grandchildren.

It was a grandson who was handling the sale. She'd had a stroke and died in hospital a few months earlier. He'd died in his own bed upstairs, days later. His death certificate gave old age as the cause of death, but the grandson said it was a broken heart, and Cassie believed he was right.

It was easily the shabbiest house she had on the books. No master en suite, no shower at all. A white melamine kitchen with a Formica work surface. It hadn't been decorated for decades and there had never, she guessed, been much money to spend on furniture or things. But love oozed from its every pore, from the very fabric of the structure, and so it was her favourite. She could try to picture herself here, and the image was comforting and warm.

He didn't want it, the brash young developer. Too much work, he said. Planning would likely nix a second floor.

She'd nodded sympathetically, as though she thought it was a shame. But she was smiling to herself as she turned the car into her own driveway, and what more could you ask from your day than that you be smiling as it drew to an end? This moment, coming home . . . This was always her favourite part.

What might she write about it, if she were selling this house? *Excellent location, close to all amenities, but still with a real feeling of rural tranquillity.* The late afternoon sunshine had bathed the mellow bricks in a coral shimmer. The cherry blossom on the weeping trees that flanked the path to the red front door were gone, but the delicate pink and white roses she'd planted around the porch when she'd moved in ten years ago were just beginning to come into bud, and elsewhere the garden was poised to run riot, demanding her attention daily. She loved this time of year. *Sunny aspect, well-established and stocked beds, charming character.* A glass of chilled Chenin Blanc, an old straw hat, her gardening clogs and something living and beautiful to tend . . . Bliss.

As she slid the gear stick into 'park' and switched off the engine, the red front door opened and he came out, as he often did, when he was working on something in the study that faced the front of the house and he heard her car.

John. Her John. The delightful man she had shared this home and the last ten years of her life with, and who had shared with her, in turn, his three teenage sons and now, their families, so that from time to time the peace here was gloriously shattered by the laughter and chatter of a crowd. The quiet, unassuming man who was fanatical about cricket and cooking curry, and growing his own vegetables in the south-facing garden, once mainly laid to lawn but now his domain. His asparagus beds, seven years in the cultivating, and his neatly netted raspberries were certainly a unique feature.

And what might she write about him? Some might say, taking in his ancient Norwegian fishing sweater, with its threadbare elbows, his thinning hair and lined face, that he could benefit from some modernising. Who couldn't? But to her he was . . .

And although an estate agent never, ever ought to use the word, here she thought it appropriate: perfect.

Grating Expectations

BY ADELE PARKS

*I*t wasn't entirely Sarah's fault that she had such specific – and high – expectations about the trip to Venice. Everyone agreed that a marriage proposal was 'more than likely'. Everyone being her mum, her sister and her four closest friends – one married, two single, one gay – a reasonable cross-section of society. At least, of Sarah's society.

After all, David and Sarah had been together for four years and three months, and they lived together, admittedly in his flat with his name on the mortgage and utility bills, but Sarah bought the groceries and she'd redecorated the place from top to bottom. That meant something.

They would be travelling club class, which was an unnecessary luxury for a short-haul flight and therefore, Sarah thought, proof positive that David wanted this to be a 'particularly special' weekend. Her preference was that he'd pop the question right at the beginning of the mini-break. Perhaps tonight? Then they could utilise the rest of the time planning the wedding or, rather more accurately, Sarah could spend the time telling David what she wanted for her big day.

She had very clear views and, frankly, little actual discussion would be required – although she'd be sensible enough to disguise that fact when the time came. She'd selected the church, venue, menu, band and bridesmaids. She had a good idea about the style of dress – but all the wedding magazines agreed you didn't really know until you actually tried on a selection. So finalising that detail would have to wait.

David wasn't into big romantic gestures so there was a reasonable chance he'd propose somewhere unsuitable, like on the plane or in a restaurant. Sarah had never liked the idea of restaurant proposals. A few of her friends' boyfriends had gone down that route and the girls always claimed to be happy enough with it, but Sarah knew she'd be put off her food and she didn't like waste. Besides, how do you hug and kiss with a table in between and everyone watching?

Sarah talked non-stop on the plane so that David wouldn't find an opportunity to ask. She chattered about the bread rolls, her ankles swelling on flights, whether it was worth sending postcards to friends and family – anything rather than have him ruin her big moment by proposing somewhere inappropriate.

They emerged from the airport and Sarah was thrilled to see a beautiful mahogany boat waiting to take them to the mainland.

Surely this private hire meant the proposal was well within reach? As they slid through the sea, the sunshine made everything appear glittery, the breeze lifted Sarah's hair and she felt like a Bond girl. Now, the boat limousine would be an ideal place to propose, she thought.

'Isn't this just perfect?' she said, staring intently and meaningfully at David.

'Bit blowy,' he replied without taking his eyes off the map.

David had an innate distrust of foreign taxi drivers and made a big deal of following their chosen route from airport to hotel so as to ensure the cabbie took the most direct path. Secretly, Sarah doubted that he had any idea how to read a map of the sea and waterways but felt it would be rude to point out as much.

It was about four o'clock by the time they dropped off their bags at the hotel. David suggested they went straight out to make the most of the late-afternoon sunshine, perhaps buy an ice cream. Sarah agreed but insisted on taking a quick shower and changing her outfit. She didn't want to be proposed to, wearing the jeans she'd travelled in. In the end it took about an hour and a half for her to shower, exfoliate, reapply make-up and select the outfit she did want to be wearing when she agreed to become Mrs Johnson.

Unfortunately, by that time the sun had slipped behind a large cloud. David grumbled and commented that stilettos were impractical footwear to forage around the uneven streets.

Sarah was in love with Venice. She'd known she would be; she'd decided it was the most romantic place in the world the moment David mentioned he'd booked a mini-break. She'd read all about Doge's Palace; for weeks now she'd imagined them strolling through St Mark's Square and taking a trip to the Accademia.

Venice did not stink; Sarah had never believed it would, despite all the grim warnings she'd had from people – like the lady in the dry cleaners, Mike from next door and the lads in the post room at her office – people who didn't have an ounce of romance in their bodies.

Mooching around the ancient back streets, they stood outside churches and wandered across umpteen pretty bridges. Despite the lines of washing flapping in the breeze, Sarah thought these streets had a shabby charm and were perfect backdrops for David to pop the big question. Clearly he did not agree. He kept resolutely silent, despite her numerous hints about how romantic everything was and how perfect. They ambled alongside the waters of St Mark's Basin. How was it described in the guidebook? A mirror to reflect the majesty and splendour of the Basilica di San Giorgio Maggiore. True enough. A perfect place for a proposal.

Sarah dawdled. She leaned her elbows on to the iron railing of a bridge and gazed out on to the canals. It was a lovely view, although she hadn't expected to be in the shade of the buildings quite so much and wished she'd worn long sleeves. In her imaginings they were always walking in the sunshine. David leaned his bum against the railings and looked in the opposite direction. Sarah tried not to be disconcerted.

'David, isn't this just so wonderful?'

Sarah gently bit her lower lip. Last week they'd been watching some chat show on TV. They'd ordered a takeaway and opened a bottle of wine. They'd chomped their way through half a box of Milk Tray, not the type of confectionery Sarah would ever take to a friend's dinner party but, in fact, their favourite. The host was interviewing Hollywood's latest hot bit of stuff who kept biting her lower lip whenever she was thinking about a question. David had been mesmerised.

'Do you have a mouth ulcer, love?' David asked.

'No, why?'

'You keep chewing your lip. I thought you were in pain. I've got some Bonjela in my wash bag. I'll dig it out for you when we get back to the hotel.'

'I don't have a mouth ulcer.'

'Maybe you've started to bite your lip as a compensation for giving up biting your nails.'

She'd always been a nail biter; David hated the habit and had often urged her to stop. She'd tried but had never gone longer than two days without caving in and having a nibble; that was until she imagined something sparkly on her third finger, left hand. Stumpy nails would so ruin the effect.

'No,' she mumbled, somewhat exasperated.

Clearly, her provocative lower-lip nibbling was doing nothing for David. She looked around for something to talk about but, despite the wealth of history, culture and bars, she was stumped. They endured a fifteen-minute silence, the first of their relationship.

Eventually David asked, 'Do you fancy something to eat? The local dish of squid pasta is supposed to be worth trying.'

'I'm tired, let's just go to bed,' and, so that he was absolutely clear, she added, 'to sleep.'

Saturday followed the same pattern. Sarah woke up hopefully and dressed in a way that she thought appropriate for accepting a proposal. David woke up bewildered and a bit resentful that a romantic mini-break in Venice hadn't culminated in even a whiff of sex. Despite the top-notch hotel with four-poster bed and everything.

His bewilderment and resentment grew as Sarah spent the day acting increasingly weirdly. Normally so relaxed and such a laugh, she'd started to behave in a way that defied belief.

Did she think he was a complete moron? He wasn't impervious to the dawdling at Kodak moments and outside jewellery windows. He knew what she wanted – she was being obvious and, frankly, her behaviour was terrifying.

He had been going to do it. Of course he had. Why not? The girl was a marvel; he adored her. Or at least he thought he adored her. But her peculiar pushy behaviour was making him . . . nervous. Suddenly, he didn't like the way she munched her food and her walk was funny, sort of lopsided. This wouldn't have been a deal-breaker under normal circumstances, but what was normal about your girlfriend holding a gun to your head, full of emotional bullets that she so clearly wanted to spend?

He'd planned to take her to Santa Maria Gloriosa dei Frari, arguably one of Venice's most sublime religious treasure troves, to see Titian's gloriously uplifting *Assumption* altar painting. He'd wanted to propose to her in front of that painting; he too was capable of assuming, planning and plotting. But her needy expectations had ruined everything. He felt she was presuming, second-guessing and, worst of all, waiting. Now he felt that he might return to England with the princess-cut diamond still in his jacket pocket.

By Sunday, they were barely speaking. Sarah insisted that she didn't want to go to a market – which was unheard of. David said he had no appetite for visiting restaurants – a first. Instead of enjoying the café orchestras, cooing pigeons and constant traffic of waiters serving alfresco diners, Sarah complained that St Mark's Square was too boisterous. She rushed towards a gondola, no longer envisaging romantic opportunities – she'd given up on that; it was Sunday evening and they were leaving early the next day – but she desperately wanted to be away from the crowds, which, as far as she could ascertain, were entirely made up of besotted lovers.

They drifted gently on a gondola, away from the crowds.

Sarah stared at the stars glistening in the navy sky

and wondered if she could be bothered to comment to David that the scene was perfect. She thought he'd ask, 'Perfect for what?' in an impatient voice, as he had every other time she'd helpfully pointed out the perfect moments on their trip. Not that there had been so many today. Of course, everything was still as interesting, as steeped in history and as culturally amazing as when they'd first arrived – only, somehow, things weren't so perfect now.

David asked the gondolier to stop singing. He whispered to Sarah that he had a headache, although she'd never known him to suffer from one before. He also muttered that the whole experience had been excruciating and a rip-off at sixty quid per person for twenty minutes' entertainment.

Sarah wondered what to do next. She supposed she'd have to finish the relationship. It was clearly going nowhere fast. She couldn't just sit around and wait for David to finally decide she was the girl for him or, worse, decide she wasn't. She had ovaries shrivelling by the minute; she didn't have unlimited time.

But she loved him so. She couldn't imagine life without him. It was all so depressing and wrong. Nothing was turning out as she'd hoped and now she could even detect unsavoury wafts from the sewer and stale sweat from the gondolier's T-shirt.

David felt miserable. Really low. He'd thought the break would be such a laugh. He'd really splashed out – good flights, cool hotel, booked the best restaurants.

Not that they'd actually honoured a booking as yet – Sarah had cried off on Friday and Saturday. He wondered if the jewellers accepted returns. What a waste. Things couldn't get any worse unless, of course, he lost the ring.

Panic! David self-frisked in a frantic attempt to track down the little box.

'What is it?' asked Sarah.

'The ring! I've lost it. On top of you being a freak, I've lost the damned ring.'

'What?'

'Sorry, I didn't mean to call you a freak.'

'That's OK. I meant the other bit. What ring?'

'An engagement ring, of course. Christ, it's dark. Can you see a ring? It cost a fortune. I can't believe this! It's in a blue box. Will you—?'

'Yes, I will.'

'—look for it!'

'Oh, right. I thought you meant—'

'I'm unlikely to propose at the moment. I've lost the ring, haven't I?' snapped David.

Sarah was already on her hands and knees. In that instant she completely forgot that she was wearing high heels and a white skirt as she groped around the damp and dark gondola floor.

Her round bottom bobbed up and down, making something shift back into place for David. Sarah no longer seemed overly keen or controlling. She was concerned and well meaning again. He loved her curvy bum and everything else about her. His gut turned.

'I'll do you a deal: if we do find the ring, I will propose, OK?'

David laughed.

'Deal. And if I like the ring I'll accept,' she added with a grin.

Extracted from Loves Me, Loves Me Not.

Ritz

BY JODI PICOULT

The note is inside the refrigerator, propped against a carton of orange juice. *I'm taking a break,* my mother has written. *Don't worry about me.*

'What's she taking a break from?' I ask out loud.

'Sanity,' my brother Devon answers. 'People don't leave notes in refrigerators.'

Devon, who is eighteen and apparently knows everything, is looking at this the wrong way, in my opinion. Granted, I'm three years younger than he is, but I think Mom has shown a peculiar genius in leaving the note between the leftovers from yesterday's lasagna and the bottle of canola oil. She knew that a message on the kitchen counter could easily be overlooked, but no matter what direction we were pulled in after school, no matter how much French verb conjugation I had to slog through, nor how many hours Devon spent making a racket with his garage band – eventually, we will give in to our growling hunger and find something to eat.

'Maybe we should call Dad,' I suggest.

A bomb would pretty much have to detonate inside

our living room to warrant a phone call to my father during business hours. He works on Wall Street, trading futures.

He leaves at four-thirty in the morning to beat the traffic going into the city from White Plains, and he gets home after seven. The irony doesn't escape me: he is so busy tracking what *might* happen that he's hardly around to enjoy the here and now.

Devon shrugs. 'She probably went out to . . . do whatever she does. You know.'

But the truth is, I have no idea what my mother does with her spare time. I mean, I guess maybe she likes to jog every now and then, or hit a good sale at a mall. I think sometimes she goes out and has lunch with one of her friends. But mostly, my vision of her is firmly planted in our house, like a vine too twined to be transplanted. Just as I used to believe that my kindergarten teacher slept underneath her desk, it is hard to picture my mother existing outside the boundaries of my home, of my life.

'She'll be back in time to make dinner,' Devon says, and then he reaches out and messes up my hair.

It is totally out of character for him – Devon is more likely to *accidentally* drop my toothbrush in the toilet than show me any sisterly affection – and somehow this compassion makes me feel worse, as if he is being nice to me in the way that people are nice to cancer patients or mentally challenged kids or anyone else who's had such bad luck that you want to compensate with kindness. I go soft inside, like the egg that my mother cooks for us when we are sick. She serves it in a little half-cup with a daisy painted on the side. I always wondered what would happen if Devon and I both got sick at once, since there is only one eggcup.

I realise, with a little shiver, that I have never seen my mother sick. I mean, sure, she gets colds and allergies, but how can someone survive over a decade without being so sick that she just crawls into bed and has someone else wait on her, hand and foot? Then again, who would fill that role for my mother? I consider what it might be like to feel lousy, but have to cook yourself your own egg and put it in the daisy cup.

And that's how I realise my mother will not be home for dinner, for breakfast – maybe not for ever.

Just so you know, I'm not stupid. I may only be in ninth grade but I get straight As; I score off the charts on the standardised tests we have to take at school. In this, I am the polar opposite of my brother, for whom school is not a journey but a condition you outgrow.

I am, however, invisible. Devon's surly enough to take up all the parenting time allotted to both of us. I hardly ever talk to my father, because he's so busy that it seems ridiculous to think he'd care about what grade I got on my science project. And my mother's usually running in a thousand directions at once. *I'll listen in a minute*, she says, but then she never quite gets around to it.

A little while after we find the note, I track Devon down in the garage, wailing on his bass while two of his friends play the drums and the guitar. This week they are calling themselves Goths in Thongs. Last week, it was the Undead Puppies.

Devon sees me and stops playing. 'What,' he says, an accusation.

'She's still not back.'

He rolls his eyes. 'Jenna, it's only been an hour.'

I cross my arms. 'I called her cell phone and she didn't answer.'

'So what? Maybe she turned it off. Maybe she's at a movie.'

'Dude,' says Yak, who plays the drums. That's not his real name, by the way. I think it's Absalom or Alistair or something like that. 'Is there a problem?'

'Our mother's gone missing.'

'Sweet,' Yak says. 'Could she take mine with her?'

I leave them alone in the garage and sit on the edge of the porch. There are flowers all along the edge of it – a net of purple and cobalt; a startling orange tiger lily, its open mouth raw and pink.

The portable phone I'm holding (just in case) rings, startling me.

'Hi,' I say breathlessly, but it is only my father. He calls every day from the station, to let my mother know which train he's catching. I think it's less about her peace of mind and more about making sure his dinner is hot when he gets home.

'Pumpkin,' he says. 'Mom around?'

'No,' I tell him. 'She left us a note—'

'Well, tell her I caught the five-fifty-eight,' he says.

'Look, Dad—'

'Gotta run, honey, if I want to make this train . . .'

He hangs up, and I let the phone fall into my lap, where it rings again almost immediately.

'Dad?' I say, picking it up.

'No,' my mother answers, 'it's me.'

'*Mom?* Where *are* you?'

In the silence, I can hear other people talking – loudspeakers, announcements I can't quite make out.

'Jenna, listen, there's meatloaf for supper,' she says. 'It's in the tinfoil on the second shelf of the fridge. You can open up a bag of salad, too.'

'You mean you won't be here for dinner?'

'Did you talk to your father?' she asks.

'He said he's catching the five-fifty-eight.' My throat closes like a fist. 'Mom, what's going on?'

For a moment, she's quiet. Then she says, 'I'll call you when I get there.'

'Get *where*?' I demand, but an electric eel of static crackles in my ear.

'Jenna,' my mother says, 'I'm losing you.'

And as the line goes dead I think, *No, it's the other way around.*

By nine o'clock at night, we are all sitting at the kitchen table, waiting for the phone to ring. My father is still wearing his dress shirt, but it's creased like a map and the sleeves are rolled up past his elbows. In front of him is the bowl of Life cereal he didn't really eat for dinner, solidifying into cement.

'Jenna,' he says, for the bazillionth time, 'you have to remember *something*.'

It figures; the one time anyone wants to listen to me, I can't remember anything important. I have already told them everything Mom said; the problem is, we really need to know what she *didn't* say.

'Could it have been an airport?' Devon asks. 'Is that what the announcements sounded like?'

'I don't know.'

My father has already called the police, but they told him that you can't file a missing persons report for twenty-four hours. And besides, it's not really a missing person if the person herself *chose* to go missing. That, the sergeant said, is just bad luck.

He scrubs his hands over his face. 'OK,' he says, as if telling himself this might make it come true.

I have been tugging at a thread on the placemat in front of me.

'Do you think it's something we did?' I ask, my voice so tiny that it rolls like a pebble to the centre of the table.

At first, I assume that nobody's heard me, or that they've ignored me, which is par for the course. But then Devon looks up.

'I forgot to fold my washing. She asked me, like, ten times, but I never got around to it. And I kind of didn't take out the trash either.' His face pinkens. 'It was *pouring*, and I knew she'd do it if I didn't, anyway.'

'I told her it was practically child abuse to make me take the late bus home after soccer practice, when she was just sitting here anyway and could come pick me up,' I admit. 'And remember when you wouldn't stop playing your stupid guitar and she was trying to balance the chequebook?'

'Maybe it wasn't just us,' Devon says and he turns to my father. 'Did you guys have a fight?'

My father scowls. 'Of course not. We barely had time to talk last week, much less fight. I was busy working on that Hashomoto deal.'

I rub a crease into the placemat with my thumb. 'Maybe it's not something we did. Maybe it's something we *didn't*.'

The phone rings, and my dad answers it on speaker phone so that we all can hear.

'Ian,' my mother says. 'Hi.'

Although we've all talked about how we're going to tiptoe around conversation when the moment actually arrives, my father completely blows it.

'Charlotte, where the hell are you?'

'San Francisco!' I can hear the smile in her voice, bright as gold. 'Can you believe it?'

'Mom?' Devon interrupts. 'Is this because of my laundry?'

My brother can be such an idiot.

'Mom,' I pipe in, only because I want her to know I'm here, too, listening. 'Is the weather nice out there?'

My father and Devon look at me as if I'm crazy.

'Charlotte,' my father says evenly, 'you've made your point. You can come back now.'

'I'm not making a point, Ian. I'm just . . . taking a vacation.'

A vacation. My mother is taking a vacation. From all of us.

'I don't understand,' my father says.

'Well, you should,' my mother replies. 'I'm doing what you do, every day: trading futures.' As soon as she hangs up, Devon dials *69.

'Good evening, the Ritz-Carlton,' a honeyed voice says. 'How may I direct your call?'

My father pushes a button and disconnects us.

'Mom's staying at the Ritz-Carlton?' I ask.

'You could cut off her credit cards,' Devon suggests. 'I saw that on *Law and Order*, once.'

'I'm not cutting off your mother's credit cards,' my father replies. 'This is just her way of going on strike.'

'Maybe we should cross the picket line, then,' Devon suggests.

'We,' my father announces, 'will hardly even notice she's gone.'

That night, we make a plan. I will be in charge of dishwashing; Devon – in spite of his lousy track record – will do the laundry. Dad will take over vacuuming and mopping of all floors. When we go to bed, the house is sparkling, perfect. Mom will come home, I think, and will be absolutely stunned.

Assuming we can keep it up.

My father comes in to tuck me in, even though he

usually doesn't do that any more. He sits down on the edge of my bed.

'Dad,' I ask. 'What do you do, for real?'

'I'm a trader, honey. You know that.'

'Yeah, but what do you *do*?'

'Say I want to buy oil for the house for next winter. I can commit now to buy it at a certain price arranged by the oil company. But maybe I have a different view about what the price of oil is going to be. Maybe I think that war will break out again, and the price of oil will rise. Maybe I think that after the election, the price will drop. My job's about hunches . . . If I think the price will be lower in the future, I can agree to sell a year from now oil that I don't own yet. If I'm right, I can buy that oil in the future and immediately resell it to the company I contracted with and make a profit. Of course, if the price of oil actually goes *higher*, I lose big time. Basically, I'm betting on the future. And I can bet it's going to get better, or I can bet it's going to get worse.'

I wonder what commodity my mother thinks she is trading in. Love? Respect? Self-confidence?

My father leans over and kisses my forehead. 'You look so much like her.'

I have heard that all my life. 'Do you really think she's just taking a vacation?'

'How could it be anything else?' my father says, but I get the feeling he's asking me, not giving me the answer.

*

Before you could see the hairline cracks in our family – when Dad was actually home for dinner; before Devon hit puberty and became the slouched, hairy, sarcastic beast that he is now; back when my mother seemed *happy* – we used to play a game at dinner. Each night we'd take turns asking a question for which there was no easy answer: *If you had a million dollars, what would you do with it? If you could change one event in history, what would it be? What would the title of your biography be, and who would you want to write it?*

I can't remember all the answers, but there were definitely some that surprised me. Like when Devon said that if he had to choose one person to have dinner with, it would be Nelson Mandela, when I would have bet my entire state quarter collection that he hadn't even known who Nelson Mandela *was*. Or when my father said that the one thing he'd take to a desert island – the only thing he needed – was not his Black-Berry, but my mother.

The one that sticks in my mind, though, was a question my mother had asked: *If you had to have amnesia for the rest of your life, and you could keep only one memory, what would it be?*

We all had a different one. My father talked about the time we all went to a Mexican restaurant and stole the balloons reserved for little kids, then sucked out the helium and sang like the Munchkins from *The Wizard of Oz*. Devon picked the time he gave me a haircut the day before my birthday – and clipped off my bangs right at the scalp. For me, it was the school play where

I was the buttercup fairy. My mother had stood up in the audience for the whole thirty seconds I was on that stage and whistled through her teeth so loud it was hard to hear the other kids with bigger parts speaking their lines.

At the time, I'd thought my mother's memory was a cop-out – not detailed enough, not specific.

'The last best one of the four of us,' she'd said.

The morning after my mother leaves us, I am the Queen of Energy. I set bowls on the table, and spoons, and a variety of cereal. I feel so helpful I can barely stand it; usually I sit down and wait for everything to be brought to me while I yawn my way into consciousness. Devon clatters into the kitchen, his hair still wet from his shower.

'I'm starving,' he says, pouring himself a mountain of Special K.

'What do you think they serve for breakfast at the Ritz?' I ask.

'It's the Ritz,' he mutters. 'They probably serve you whatever you want.'

'Waffles?'

'With whipped cream and strawberries.'

'Omelettes,' I say. 'Made to order.'

Devon snorts. 'Special K. Except it's *more* special there.' He reaches for the milk and shakes it. 'Is there any more in the fridge?'

'No.'

'Well, this is empty.'

'It's not my fault,' I shoot back.

'What else is there to eat?'

'How am I supposed to know?'

We both stop arguing; this is usually the moment where Mom turns around at the stove and tells us to do that very same thing. Devon reaches across the table for the carton of orange juice and pours it over his cereal.

'What?' he accuses, when I stare at him. 'It's orange juice plus calcium. That's practically milk.'

Last week, during dinner, Devon had announced he doesn't want to go to college. He wants to travel the world with his band, go build huts on a tropical island, *find* himself. My father had hit the ceiling at this announcement. *You couldn't find yourself with both hands free*, he said. *You want to find yourself? Do it with a good, liberal arts education.* Devon had lashed out like a bear caught in a trap he hadn't seen coming.

How could Dad know anything about the world when he hadn't seen anything but the inside of the New York Mercantile Exchange for the past twenty years?

By now, my father's come downstairs. He smells like the weekend: shampoo and fresh-cut grass and after-shave on his cheeks.

'So!' he says, too brightly. 'What's for breakfast?'

I picture Mom eating her Belgian waffle in bed.

After the fight with Devon, my father had turned to my mother: *Charlotte, tell him I'm right.*

I try, but I can't remember what she said.

*

Three days after my mother leaves us, we realise that the vacuum cleaner is missing. What's really unfortunate about this is that we make the discovery after Devon has knocked over a spider plant – and all its soil – onto the living room rug.

Four days after she leaves us, we give up trying to cook a meal and get all its bits and pieces – meat, potatoes, vegetables – on the table at once; instead, we order in pizza.

At school, I've had to make excuses – *the reason my mother can't come to the Art Open House is because she's visiting her sister; she didn't sign my independent reading sheet because she's gone to a conference on Sanibel Island.* The only person who knows the truth is my best friend, Nuala. I can trust her implicitly; I swear I could tell her I'm a hermaphrodite and she wouldn't even blink. When I said that my mother had left, she asked if it was an affair, something that I hadn't even *thought* of.

One day Nuala comes into homeroom with an article she's printed off the Internet.

'Check this out,' she says. 'Someone did a study on stay-at-home moms and figured out what their salary would be if they had one.'

I scan the article. Basically, the salary was a compilation of real jobs, pro-rated:

Twenty-two hours of being a housekeeper, fifteen hours of being a day-care-centre teacher, 13.6 hours of being a chef, right on down to van driver (4.7 hours) and psychologist (3.9 hours). They figured in overtime pay, because it was a ninety-one-hour week. If my mom was working for a company, instead of us, she'd be making $134,121 a year.

'That's a *lot*,' I say.

Nuala folds the paper and sticks it in her backpack again.

'It's only a lot if you actually get paid,' she said.

That night, I can't sleep. I pad downstairs in my bare feet to the kitchen. It is now Devon's job to wash the dishes, but he's been playing with his band after school and so there's a stack of bowls in the sink that's precariously curved, like a clock tower in a Dr Seuss book. A round of melon on the cutting board has flies crawling across its belly.

Someone's left the milk out. Again.

It isn't until my father speaks, in a hushed whisper, that I even realise he's sitting at the kitchen table with the phone pressed up to his ear.

'It will be different,' he says. 'I promise.'

I hear phrases snipped from their sentences: *taken for granted, because, without you.* I try not to listen. Instead, I think of all the things that fall apart when you remove their core: a head of lettuce; a solar system; a household like ours.

There is a muffled beep: my father hanging up the phone. I am just about to back out of the kitchen when he says, 'How much of that did you hear?'

'Nothing,' I lie.

I sit down across from him at the table.

258

'She left once before,' my father says.

He couldn't have surprised me more if he'd announced that my mother used to be a trapeze artist in the circus.

'I don't remember that.'

'That's because you and Devon were babies.' My father looks up at me. 'She was gone for three months.'

Three months?

I can feel the question that I've wanted to ask all this time, filling me like a hot-air balloon, so that I burst at the seams. 'Didn't she love us?'

'*So* much,' my father says. 'So much that she started to forget who she used to be.'

My eyes start to burn. What I haven't told anyone – not Nuala, not Devon, not my dad – is what I think about when it's just me and the stoic moon alone in my room at night. That if I'd been a better daughter – prettier, smarter, funnier – she might have had reason to stay.

'Can't you go get her?' I beg. 'Can't you just bring her back?'

My father puts his hand over mine.

'That's what I did the first time, when she'd been gone a week. And she ran away again.' He shakes his head. 'You can't force a wind to blow the way you want it to, Jenna. You have to hope it gets there on its own.'

He leaves me sitting in the dark, and I guess I fall asleep there, because I dream about my mother. She is in the circus, wearing a sparkly bodysuit, her hair pulled back into a ballerina's bun. I see the cloud of chalk rising from her palms as she climbs a ladder hung on the rungs of real stars. I think of what it must feel like to fly.

And then, I can see the rest of us. We're all miles below, looking up. We're connected to her by the thinnest of strings – spider-silk, gossamer – nearly invisible, unless you happen to be the ones tethering her to the ground.

The second week after my mother leaves us, I start missing appointments. My father is at work, and although Devon is supposed to drive me to my orthodontist appointment, he forgets and stays late at Yak's house, writing a heavy metal ballad.

Instead of relying on Devon to pick me up after soccer practice, I take my bike and ride home five miles every night. I have never been so strong, or in such good shape. I imagine my mother looking at me when she comes home, and being impressed. *It's all because of you*, I will say.

Don't think she's neglecting us. Every night at seven o'clock, she calls. We talk like ordinary mothers and daughters, as if it is perfectly normal for her to be living in a hotel thousands of miles away. She tells us all about San Francisco. She talks about the hotel: slippers left beside the bed during turndown service; about the exercise room staffed with people who bring you cups of cold water while you're on the treadmill; about how, when you call the front desk, they say, *Yes, Mrs*

Hamilton, what can we do for you, as if you are the only guest in the entire hotel.

'Wow,' I say. 'It sounds amazing.'

'Tell me about your day,' she'll say. 'How was your French test? Did you win your soccer game?'

I answer, and then I ask her when she's coming home.

On the sixteenth day, she says, 'Why don't you come get me?'

It really shouldn't be this easy to slip away. Flying is out of the question, of course. Even if I had the money or the means to get to an airport, I couldn't get on a plane as an unaccompanied minor. But here's an interesting fact: you only have to be fifteen to travel alone on a bus. And I can get to San Francisco in twenty-two hours.

I know where my father keeps his spare cash – Devon let me in on that secret two years ago. It's in the left dress shoe he wears when he puts on his tuxedo, which is never, which is why it's a good place to store money. I feel guilty taking it all ($546.93) so I conservatively borrow two hundred dollars. The Greyhound ticket costs only $88.50. No matter how expensive the cabs are in San Francisco, I'll still have enough to get to the Ritz.

On the bus I sit next to an old woman who seems convinced I'm a teenage runaway. *If only you knew*, I think. I make up this story about how my mother and father are divorced; how my mom is sick and needs my help, and how I have a crippling fear of planes and have to travel this way. There is so much garbage coming out of my mouth that I might as well be littering the whole bus. But, amazingly, the woman buys it. She even gives me the potholder she's crocheted on the journey, as a special gift to boost my mother's spirits.

I'm tired when I arrive – number one, it's four-thirty in the morning; number two, I've had to transfer buses twice – and I'm sure I look worse than I did when I had the stomach flu for a whole week, but the doorman still opens the door of the taxi as if I am royalty.

'Checking in, miss?' he asks, and he directs me up the elevators to reception.

The lobby is a marble palace; an arrangement of flowers I have never even seen in books before rises like a fountain spray from a table in the centre. Somewhere, there's a fountain; the water rushes like a river. It smells like jasmine, like peace.

With my knapsack hiked on my shoulders I walk up to the front desk. I am almost expecting them to greet me by name, as my mother says they do when she calls downstairs, but then again, why would they know me yet?

'I'm here to see my mother,' I say. 'Mrs Hamilton?'

The woman behind the desk has olive skin and a smile as neat and even as a string of pearls. 'Is she expecting you?'

'Sort of,' I mumble, but by then the woman is calling my mother's room.

I can't really remember the next few minutes. All I

know is that almost as soon as the phone is hung back up again, the elevator behind me chimes and then there's something I've almost forgotten – the vanilla tones of her perfume, mixed with the sweet scent of the miracle you've been waiting for. My face fits into the curve of her neck, just as it did when I was little, and her arms close around me like a safety net. I can't even speak; as it turns out, there aren't words for when you're so full of light you think you might explode or faint or scream, or maybe all three.

'Oh, Jenna. I missed you so much,' my mother cries. She glances over my head at the lobby around us. 'Where's Devon? And your dad?'

I blink. 'In White Plains.'

She draws away, her face flushed. 'Are you telling me,' she says, and then she swallows, as if the words rose too quickly in her throat. 'Are you telling me you came here from New York all by yourself?'

'Well,' I point out, 'you *told* me to come get you.'

'I meant *all* of you!' my mother cries. 'Including an adult! Don't tell me your father let you—'

'He doesn't know I'm here.'

She takes a step backwards, as if I've slapped her. 'For God's sake, Jenna, what were you thinking? You could have gotten lost, or hurt, or—'

'So could you!' I shout. 'You, of all people, have no right to tell me what to do!'

We are both shocked; I don't think I've ever heard myself yell so loud. I'm supposed to be the quiet one, the one who never speaks, or at least the one who never makes herself heard.

My mother's cheeks bloom; there's a colour for shame. 'I'm your *mother*.'

'Oh, really? What kind of mother leaves her family to go live at a Ritz-Carlton? You don't get to be a mother part-time, when you feel like it. It's all or nothing.'

By now, my face is flushed, too; my eyes are stinging. It wasn't supposed to be like this.

The way I'd planned it in my mind, my mother would be so overjoyed to have me here that she wouldn't be able to let me out of her sight, much less her arms. The way I'd planned it, there was no screaming involved.

My mother stares at me for a long moment and then she reaches for my hand.

She draws me toward the elevator and only when we're inside, alone, does she start talking again.

'I just wanted to know what it could have been like,' she says softly.

'What?'

The elevator doors open, and she faces me. 'Someone else's life,' she answers.

As soon as we reach her room, she calls my father. There's no answer, but it's early – he and Devon could easily sleep through the ringing of the phone.

'We'll try again a little later,' she says, but I am too busy looking around.

The bed, wide as an ocean, is dressed in white. An overstuffed chair sits across from the mahogany desk. In the bathroom I can just make out the jutting lip of a marble tub the colour of sandstone.

'I don't make the bed,' my mother says. 'I don't clean the bathroom. I don't have to cook. I don't have do anything, and it magically gets done.'

It is, I realise, the way I've lived my whole life.

After I take a shower, I wrap a thick white robe around myself and towel dry my hair. My mother is propped up in bed, watching CNN.

'Do you always watch the news?' I ask.

She turns to me. 'Sometimes. Why?'

I shrug. 'I guess I just wanted to know what you do when I leave for school.'

My mother grins. 'I curl up near the door like a puppy, Jenna, and wait until you come home.'

'Yeah, right.' I hesitate. 'Did you ever want to be anything else?'

'What do you mean?'

'Like, I don't know, join the circus. Or work in an office, like Dad. Anything.'

'I majored in zoology in college,' she says. 'I had this vision of going to track elephant migration in Africa.'

My mother? In *Africa*?

'You don't even like *camping*.'

'Yeah, well, the dreams are always different from the reality, aren't they?' She laughs. 'Anyway, I met your father, and suddenly Africa seemed very far away.'

Suddenly, I remember what my mother said after

the fight about Devon not going to college. When my father asked her to talk sense at my brother, she stood up and asked if anyone wanted more broccoli.

'You think Devon should travel,' I say.

My mother sighs. 'Maybe. Or go work for the Peace Corps or fall in love with a woman from Somalia or play at the Cavern Club in Liverpool. I don't know what he *should* do. I just know what he *shouldn't*.' She glances up. 'He shouldn't wake up one day when he's forty-three and wonder what it looks like in Bangladesh or Bali, or if the toilets really flush in the opposite direction in Australia. I guess I just wish . . . I wish I had spent a little more time in the world.'

It occurs to me that there are Ritz-Carltons in every corner of the planet. That this might not be a break for my mother, but a beginning. What if it turns out I didn't come here to bring her back, but to say goodbye?

'You must be exhausted,' my mother says. 'Why don't you go to sleep?'

I want to tell her that I'm fine, that I don't have to sleep at all, but suddenly I am so tired that I can't even form the words. I fit my curves against hers, as if we are carved from the same stone.

When Devon and I were little we used to put on gymnastics shows on the front lawn. Sometimes, when a somersault came out wobbly or a cartwheel landed wrong, we'd shout out, *Do over!* This was the cue for Mom, who was the audience, to pretend that the first one had never happened.

'If you could,' I ask, 'would you start over?'

Not only does my mother listen, she understands what I'm asking. She reaches across me to turn out the light; it feels like an embrace.

'No,' she answers. 'I wouldn't have missed you for the world.'

For a moment when I wake up, I think I've died. I have a cloud drawn up to my chin; the world is washed in the watercolours of early morning. Then I remember where I am, where *we* are, and I focus on the insistent knocking on the door. My mother wraps the terrycloth robe around herself, pulls open the door and falls into my father's arms.

Then she lets go so that she can gather Devon beneath her wing; and from the way he clutches her, it's hard to believe this is the same brother who barely acknowledges her when his friends are around, because it's uncool to have a mother, I guess. Instead, he grabs onto her – awkward, because he's bigger than she is by now – and, if I am not mistaken, he might be crying.

Meanwhile, my father's spied me. He stumbles in an effort to get closer and crawls onto the bed to wrap me in his arms.

'If you ever run away again,' he threatens, the words muffled into my hair, 'I will kill you.' But he's holding me so tight, I know he couldn't possibly mean it.

I wonder if *this* is why people run away – not because

they want to *get* anywhere, but because they need to remember what they'd miss if they left for good.

Devon eats a waffle with strawberries and whipped cream; I have oatmeal and raisin toast and tea poured out of a little pot just for me. It would be great to get a little china teapot like this, even just to use in our boring old house. Maybe then it wouldn't be quite so boring.

'We don't have to go home just yet,' my father says. 'The only times I've been to San Francisco, I've been stuck in business meetings. I haven't really seen anything.'

He has apologised to my mother, and my mother has apologised to him. Or something like that. They spent a long time with their arms around each other, their whispered words a screen. It reminded me of the wild animals you see on HD television channels, the ones who find a long-lost pack member and nuzzle and circle and huddle close for days, lest the other one disappear again.

There is quiet music in the restaurant and women stroll across the lobby, their high heels kissing the marble. Businessmen hold folded newspapers beneath their arms and talk in languages I don't understand. A waiter comes by with a fresh glass of orange juice for my father, before he's even finished his first.

'Maybe we should *all* move in here,' he jokes.

I listen to my family talk about how to spend the day, all the possibilities. And I cannot remember the last time we did this: made choices as a unit, instead of individuals.

I set my spoon on the edge of my oatmeal bowl. 'What person,' I ask quietly, 'would you most want to trade places with?'

At first, everyone keeps talking, and I figure they haven't heard me. But then, one by one, they stop speaking. I bet they're all going to laugh – it was one thing to play games at the table when we were younger, but now? I might as well have IDIOT written on my forehead.

'Bill Gates,' my father says. 'For all the obvious reasons.'

Devon is next. 'Brad Pitt. *Helloooo*, Angelina.'

We look at my mother, it's her turn. 'No one,' she says, smiling. 'There isn't a single person who's got it better than me right now.'

I almost want to let her know, at that moment, that she was wrong all those years ago about the memory you'd keep. It isn't the last best one you want to save; it's the one you haven't had yet. But I'll have years to explain that. And I'll have a lifetime to prove that even if an exotic destination has dazzling culture, stunning scenery and spectacular hotels, there's something it can never be: your home.

My mother and father and brother, they're all looking at me. I can't remember the last time anyone was hanging on my words. I recall what I thought last night, when I first saw my mother: what if it turns out this isn't about going back, but starting over?

What if?

I open my mouth, and I tell them what they're waiting to hear.

Ritz is also available in a longer version as a Kindle Single ebook entitled *Leaving Home: Short Fiction by Jodi Picoult*.

The Wrong Category

BY RUTH RENDELL

*T*here hadn't been a killing now for a week. The evening paper's front page was devoted instead to the economic situation and an earthquake in Turkey. But page three kept up the interest in this series of murders. On it were photographs of the six victims, all recognisably belonging to the same type. There, in every case, although details of features naturally varied, were the same large liquid eyes, full soft mouth and long dark hair.

Barry's mother looked up from the paper. 'I don't like you going out at night.'

'What, me?' said Barry.

'Yes, you. All these murders happened round here. I don't like you going out after dark. It's not as if you have to, it's not as if it's for work.' She got up and began to clear the table, but continued to speak in a low whining tone. 'I wouldn't say a word if you were a big chap. If you were the size of your cousin Ronnie, I wouldn't say a word. A fellow your size doesn't stand a chance against that maniac.'

'I see,' said Barry. 'And whose fault is it that I'm

only five feet two? I might just point out that a woman of five feet who marries a bloke only two inches taller can't expect to have giants for kids. Right?'

'I sometimes think you only go roving about at night, doing what you want, to prove you're as big a man as your cousin Ronnie.'

Barry thrust his face close up to hers. 'Look, leave off, will you?' He waved the paper at her. 'I might not have the height, but I'm not in the right category. Has that occurred to you? Has it?'

'All right, all right. I wish you wouldn't be always shouting.'

In his bedroom, Barry put on his new velvet jacket and dabbed cologne on his wrists and neck. He looked spruce and dapper. His mother gave him an apprehensive glance as he passed her on his way to the back door, and returned to her contemplation of the pictures in the newspaper. Six of them in two months. The girlish faces, doe-eyed, diffident, looked back at her or looked aside or stared at distant unknown objects. After a while she folded the paper and switched on the television. Barry, after all, was not in the right category, and that must be her comfort.

He liked to go and look at the places where the bodies of the victims had been found. It brought him a thrill of danger and a sense of satisfaction. The first of them had been strangled very near his home on a path, which first passed between draggled allotments, then became an alley plunging between the high brown wall of a convent and the lower red-brick wall of a school.

Barry took this route to the livelier part of the town, walking rapidly but without fear, and pausing at the point – a puddle of darkness between lamps – where the one they called Pat Leston had died. It seemed to him, as he stood there, that the very atmosphere, damp, dismal and silent, breathed evil and the horror of the act.

He appreciated it, inhaled it, and then passed on to seek, on the waste ground, the common, in a deserted back street of condemned houses, those other murder scenes. After the last killing they had closed the underpass, and Barry found to his disappointment that it was still closed.

He had walked a couple of miles and had hardly seen a soul. People stayed at home. There was even some kind of panic, he had noticed, when it got to six and the light was fading and the buses and tube trains were emptying themselves of the last commuters. In pairs they scurried. They left the town as depopulated as if a plague had scoured it.

Entering the high street, walking its length, Barry saw no one, apart from those protected by the metal and glass of motor vehicles, as well as an old woman hunched on a step. Bundled in dirty clothes, a scarf over her head and a bottle in her hand, she was as safe as he – as far, or farther, from the right category.

But he was still on the watch. Next to viewing the spots where the six had died, he best enjoyed singling out the next victim. No one, for all the boasts of the newspapers and the policemen, knew the type as well as he did. Slight and small-boned, long-legged, sway-backed, with huge eyes, pointed features and long dark hair. He was almost sure he had selected the Italian one as a potential victim some two weeks before the event, though he could never be certain.

So far today he had seen no one likely, in spite of watching with fascination the exit from the tube on his own way home. But now, as he entered the Red Lion and approached the bar, his eye fell on a candidate who corresponded to the type more completely than anyone he had yet singled out. Excitement stirred in him. But it was unwise, with everyone so alert and nervous, to be caught staring. The barman's eyes were on him. He asked for a half of lager, paid for it, tasted it and, as the barman returned to rinsing glasses, turned slowly to appreciate to the full that slenderness, that soulful timid look, those big expressive eyes, and that mane of black hair.

But things had changed during the few seconds his back had been turned. Previously he hadn't noticed that there were two people in the room, another as well as the candidate, and now they were sitting together. From intuition, at which Barry fancied himself as adept, he was sure the girl had picked the man up. There was something in the way she spoke as she lifted her full glass that convinced him, something in her look, shy yet provocative.

He heard her say, 'Well, thank you, but I didn't mean to . . .' and her voice trailed away, drowned by the other's brashness.

'Catch my eye? Think nothing of it, love. My pleasure. Your fella one of the unpunctual sort, is he?'

She made no reply. Barry was fascinated, compelled to stare, by the resemblance to Pat Leston, by more than that: by seeing in this face what seemed a quintessence, a gathering together and a concentrating here of every quality variously apparent in each of the six. And what gave it a particular piquancy was to see it side by side with such brutal ugliness. He wondered at the girl's nerve, her daring to make overtures. And now she was making them afresh, actually laying a hand on his sleeve.

'I suppose you've got a date yourself?' she said.

The man laughed. 'Afraid I have, love. I was just whiling away ten minutes.' He started to get up.

'Let me buy you a drink.'

His answer was only another harsh laugh. Without looking at the girl again, he walked away and through the swing doors out into the street. That people could expose themselves to such danger in the present climate of feeling intrigued Barry, his eyes now on the girl, who was also leaving the pub. In a few seconds it was deserted, the only clients likely to visit it during that evening all gone.

A strange idea, with all its amazing possibilities, crossed his mind and he stood on the pavement, gazing the length of the High Street. But the girl had crossed the road and was waiting at the bus stop, while the man was only just visible in the distance, turning into the entrance of the underground car park.

Barry banished the idea, ridiculous, perhaps, and, to him, rather upsetting. He crossed the road behind the oncoming bus, wondering how to pass the rest of the evening. Review once more those murder scenes, was all that suggested itself to him, and then go home.

It must have been the wrong bus for her. She was still waiting. And as Barry approached, she spoke to him. 'I saw you in the pub.'

'Yes,' he said. He never knew how to talk to girls. They intimidated and irritated him, especially when they were taller than he, and most of them were. The little thin ones he despised.

'I thought,' she said hesitantly, 'I thought I was going to have someone to see me home.'

Barry made no reply. She came out of the bus shelter, quite close to him, and he saw that she was much bigger and taller than he had thought at first.

'I must have just missed my bus. There won't be another for ten minutes.' She looked, and then he looked, at the shiny desert of this shopping centre, lighted and glittering and empty, pitted with the dark holes of doorways and passages. 'If you're going my way,' she said, 'I thought maybe . . .'

'I'm going through the path,' he said. Round there, that was what everyone called it, the path.

'That'll do me.' She sounded eager and pleading. 'It's a short cut to my place. Is it all right if I walk along with you?'

'Suit yourself,' he said. 'One of them got killed down there. Doesn't that bother you?'

She only shrugged.

They began to walk along together up the yellow and white glazed street, not talking, at least a yard apart. It was a chilly damp night, and a gust of wind caught them as, past the shops, they entered the path. The wind blew out the long red silk scarf she wore and she tucked it back inside her coat. Barry never wore a scarf, though most people did at this time of the year. It amused him to notice just how many did, as if they had never taken in the fact that all those six had been strangled with their own scarves.

There were lamps in this part of the path, attached by iron brackets to the red wall and the brown. Her sharp-featured face looked greenish in the light, and gaunt, and scared. Suddenly he wasn't intimidated by her any more or afraid to talk to her.

'Most people,' he said, 'wouldn't walk down here at night for a million pounds.'

'You do,' she said. 'You were coming down here alone.'

'And no one gave me a million,' he said cockily. 'Look, that's where the first one died, just round this corner.'

She glanced at the spot expressionlessly and walked on ahead of Barry. He caught up with her. If she hadn't been wearing high heels she wouldn't have been that much taller than he. He pulled himself up to his full height, stretching his spine, as if effort and desire could make him as tall as his cousin Ronnie.

'I'm stronger than I look,' he said. 'A man's always stronger than a woman. It's the muscles.'

He might not have spoken for all the notice she took. The walls ended and gave way to low railings behind which the allotments, scrubby plots of cabbage stumps and waterlogged weeds, stretched away. Beyond them, but a long way off, rose the backs of tall houses hung with wooden balconies and iron staircases. A pale moon had come out and cast over this dismal prospect a thin, cold radiance.

'There'll be someone killed here next,' he said. 'It's just the place. No one to see. The killer could get away over the allotments.'

She stopped and faced him. 'Don't you ever think about anything but those murders?'

'Crime interests me. I'd like to know why he does it.' He spoke insinuatingly, his resentment of her driven away by the attention she was at last giving him. 'Why d'you think he does it? It's not for money or sex. What's he got against them?'

'Maybe he hates them.' Her own words seemed to frighten her and, strangely, she pulled off the scarf, which the wind had again been flapping, and thrust it into her coat pocket. 'I can understand that.' She looked at him with a mixture of dislike and fear. 'I hate men, so I can understand it,' she said, her voice trembling and shrill. 'Come on, let's walk.'

'No.' Barry put out his hand and touched her arm. His fingers clutched her coat sleeve. 'No, you can't just leave it there. If he hates them, why does he?'

'Perhaps he's been turned down too often,' she said, backing away from him. 'Perhaps a long time ago one of them hurt him. He doesn't want to kill them, but he can't help himself.' As she flung his hand off her arm the words came spitting out. 'Or he's just ugly. Or little, like you.'

Barry stood on tiptoe to bring himself to her height. He took a step towards her, his fists up. She backed against the railings and a long shudder went through her. Then she wheeled away and began to run, stumbling because her heels were high. It was those heels, or the roughness of the ground, or the new darkness as clouds dimmed the moon, that brought her down.

Collapsed in a heap, with one shoe kicked off, she slowly raised her head and looked into Barry's eyes. He made no attempt to touch her. She struggled to her feet, wiped her grazed and bleeding hand on the scarf and immediately, without a word, they were locked together in the dark.

Several remarkable features distinguished this murder from the others. There was blood on the victim, who had fair hair instead of dark, though otherwise strongly resembling Patrick Leston and Dinno Facci. Apparently, since Barry Halford had worn no scarf, the murderer's own had been used.

But ultimately it was the evidence of a slim, dark-haired customer of the Red Lion that led the police to the conclusion that the killer of these seven young men was a woman.

Black Rock

BY LOUISE SHARLAND

*T*ess watched, transfixed, as the retreating tide sucked Michael deeper and deeper into the waterlogged sand. His tiny feet had disappeared under a mass of pulverised seashells and he was now struggling to maintain his recently acquired balance.

'Mama!' he squealed, his soft bleat a mixture of both fear and delight.

'There you go, little man,' said Tess, plucking her son from the water's grip. 'Safe and sound. Shall we go find your sister?'

A short way along the beach, Anna was busily decorating a sandcastle with an assortment of plastic bottle tops and metal ring-pulls. Two ice-lolly sticks, held together in a cross shape by a pink hair bobble, had been placed prominently on the top turret.

'Is this where the princess sleeps?' asked Tess, kneeling down beside her.

'No!' snapped Anna, disgusted at her mother's ignorance. 'It's Daddy's room!'

Tess closed her eyes and forced herself to breathe. She remembered suddenly her gloriously tuxedoed father, standing next to her in the archway of a country church, only moments before he would escort her into a future life.

'Always count to ten, love,' he whispered, as the bridesmaids fussed behind her. 'Before you bite back, always count to ten.' Then, kissing her softly on both cheeks, he added, 'It worked a treat on your mum, and I'm sure it will do the same for your Adam.'

Michael sneezed, pulling her back into the present.

'Anna,' said Tess softly. 'Your d—'

'I know!' the little girl growled, refusing even to look at her mother. 'You don't have to remind me!'

Tess had reached the count of eight by the time she heard the jangle of chimes.

'Why don't we get an ice cream?'

'That would be lovely, Mummy,' said Anna, and although she was smiling, her grey eyes were flat.

They had walked only a few metres when the little girl stopped.

'Just a minute!' she cried and, turning, raced back towards the castle.

By now, the tide had forced its way through her carefully constructed barricade and was slowly sweeping its way up to the tiny drawbridge she had constructed out of driftwood and a piece of dental floss Tess had found in the bottom of her beach bag.

'I need to double-check!' Anna called, her voice breathy and verging on frantic.

Lately, Anna had needed to double-check a lot of things: that the front door was locked, that the cooker was turned off, that Michael was properly secured in his car seat. Each time, Tess would smile and reassure her daughter that everything was going to be all right. A creeping sense of helplessness remained, however, threatening to engulf her like a tsunami over a break-water. Now, as she gazed out at the sun-bleached horizon, Tess forced herself to focus on the neoprene-clad surfers and pray for the panic to pass.

'I just want to make sure it doesn't blow over,' whispered Anna, gently pushing the lolly cross deeper into the sand.

'But, darling, the tide will—'

'It's all right, Mummy. I want the water to have it.'

They walked silently to the ice-cream van parked next to the lifeguard station and waited patiently in the long queue of summer holidaymakers.

'Choc-o-lat, choc-o-lat,' gurgled Michael, his face alight with the prospect of ice cream twice in one day.

'One chocolate cone and one Calippo, please,' said Tess to the young man serving, and turning to her daughter asked, 'What flavour would you like, darling?'

'I want coffee flavour, please,' said Anna, hands firmly on hips.

'But you don't like—' began Tess, but something about the way her daughter stood before her, so deter-mined and yet so vulnerable, made her relent, even though she knew the three-pound ice-cream cone would go untouched.

By late afternoon the wind had shifted and the children, both cold and tired, were persuaded to return to the caravan. They packed up their sand-encrusted swimming costumes and flattened juice cartons, and slowly negotiated their way across the cove just as the first fat drops of rain fell. Clouds of India ink reeled towards them and in the distance they could hear deep rumblings.

'Funder!' shrieked Michael, shifting excitedly from foot to foot. 'Funder, funder!'

'I like thunder, I like rain,' sang Anna, grabbing her brother by the hands and swinging him around wildly. 'But I hate Michael, he's a pain!'

'Macs on!' ordered Tess, quickly zipping the children into compliance. 'We don't want to get wet, do we?'

'But Mummy,' said Anna, a look of bewilderment creasing her delicate features, 'we've been swimming all day.'

Blue waters changed to grey, as frothy, white-topped waves arched furiously towards the shore. Tess felt the pull, could hear their song, reminding her again of Adam and the time he had playfully dared her to look over the precipice at Beachy Head.

'Once your arms held me, they held me so tight,' she had joked, rising to his challenge. 'But the whispering waters will hold me tonight.'

The first crack of thunder made them all scream and race back towards the cove for shelter.

'We'll just stay here a minute,' whispered Tess, desperately trying to decide if it would be safer to risk being struck by lightning or falling rocks. Across the bay, great neon streaks sliced their way through meaty rain clouds.

'This is brilliant!' yelled Anna, her eyes aglow. 'Absolutely brilliant!'

Rainwater coursed its way down worried grooves of stone, bringing with it a glistening array of tiny mineral treasures.

'Mummy, look, look!' screamed Anna.

In her hand she held an incisor-shaped piece of black rock, a glossy tooth of flint spat out from the decaying cliff face above.

'A monster's tooth,' laughed Tess, 'or maybe a dinosaur's!'

Anna's eyes widened and then, pursing her lips, she carefully placed the artefact in the inside pocket of her mac before casting her eyes to the ground once again.

'Do you think there are any more?'

'Maybe, darling, but I really think it's time to go.' Next to her, Michael trembled, but Anna positively hummed. 'We can come back again tomorrow . . .'

'No!' screamed the little girl and, dropping to her knees, began scraping her fingernails through the wet sand. 'I need to find another one!'

'Anna, stop it!'

Tess tried lifting her daughter with one hand while holding on to her terrified son with the other. Finally, in desperation, she grabbed Anna by the back of her mac and yanked her roughly to her feet.

'We're going, now!'

The trek across the open beach seemed endless.

Michael cowered in his mother's arms, his sodden curls flattened against his forehead, while Anna sulked silently behind them. By the time they reached the caravan, the little boy's lips were blue.

'In the shower, both of you,' called Tess, stripping the children and leaving their soaking clothes in a pile by the front door. 'Let Michael go first, Anna, his teeth are chattering.'

She waited until they were both in the shower before letting the tears come. What would Adam have made of it all? she thought, resting her burning forehead against the cool of the windowpane.

'You're mad as always, woman!'

It was as if the voice was beside her and for a moment Tess forgot.

'Adam?' she whispered. 'Are you there?'

The response was silence.

She sat the children in front of the electric fire as she applied Michael's eczema cream and ran a comb through Anna's long, fine hair.

'When you were very little you used to scream and cry when I did your hair,' Tess recalled. 'Daddy was the only one you'd let near you with a comb.'

'I was afraid,' Anna murmured.

'What?'

'If I screamed or cried, Daddy would be cross with me.'

Tess put down the comb.

'He loved you very much, Anna. You know that, don't you?'

The little girl nodded.

Say something, pleaded Tess silently, but as always her daughter's anguish seemed inaccessible.

'Hungry!' cried Michael. 'I have crisps?'

'No, you cannot have crisps,' replied Tess and, getting up, kissed both children before heading towards the kitchenette to make tea.

Removing the half-empty bottle of Pinot from the refrigerator, she poured herself a glass and took a large sip.

'You two can watch *Finding Nemo* again while I cook dinner,' she called and, refilling her glass, slid the fish fingers under the grill.

Tess hadn't even got halfway through *We're Going on a Bear Hunt* before both children were fast asleep. She didn't have the energy to carry them to bed, so instead covered them in clean towels and let them snooze on the settee. Downing the last of the Pinot, she picked up her beach bag and headed for the door. Outside, dusk was creeping in; the sky washed clean except for a few jagged streaks of fuchsia.

'Nice day tomorrow,' she mumbled.

Sitting down on the metal steps, she began rummaging through her bag for the secret refuge she kept hidden there: her coveted package of menthol-tipped cigarettes. Adam had hated her smoking, putting his foot down and demanding she quit when she first became pregnant with Anna. Now that she was on her own, however, the sense of something between her lips, between her fingertips, was strangely comforting.

'Where are you, you little b—?'

She felt something jam under her fingernails and grimaced as she remembered Michael tipping a spade full of sand into her bag that morning.

'Dammit!'

Bit by bit, Tess removed the contents of her bag – purse, sun cream, Michael's inhaler – and laid them on the ground in front of her. Finding her cigarettes at last, she lit one, took a deep drag and carried on – mobile, wet wipes, car keys. Finally, she lifted the empty bag and tipped the sand into her hand. It was pale, speckled, unremarkable. She let it run through her fingers and sprinkle her toes. It smelled of seaweed and, when she touched her tongue to the few tiny grains that still clung to her palm, tasted surprisingly bland.

Back home in Hereford, there was a tiny glass bottle filled with sand. That sand was different: dark and grimy, it tasted of musty places and something else she couldn't quite identify. It had been there since last Easter, not long after the Army Casualty Officer had dropped off Adam's personal effects. Inside the plain brown box there were no surprises – family photos, wash bag, iPod – but when she had unrolled the sleeves of Adam's favourite denim shirt, the fine, dark powder had scattered across the dining-room table. She found it everywhere – in his socks, trainers, underpants, even between the pages of the best-seller she had bought him for Christmas.

The combat dust, as she began to call it, was

carefully decanted into an old perfume bottle, wrapped in pink tissue paper and then placed at the back of her sock drawer, hidden away like some magical talisman too dangerous for the human eye to see.

The sound of laughter made Tess glance over to the caravan opposite, where a lively family game of charades was taking place. Sighing deeply, she returned her possessions to her bag, wiped her hands clean and went back inside.

It was dark now and she felt numb with fatigue, but she still had the children to get to bed. Michael was easy – small and lightweight, he even hooked his legs around his mother's waist as she carried him to the tiny third bedroom. Anna, always a troubled sleeper, flailed and stiffened as Tess tried to hoist her on to her shoulder. Even though she had a room of her own, she had insisted on sleeping with her mother and Tess, desperate for a connection of any kind, had relented.

'There, there,' whispered Tess, laying her daughter on the cool sheets. 'Sleep tight now, darl—'

From beneath her daughter's pillow jutted something hard and angular. Carefully, Tess slid her hand in and removed the object. It was a picture frame, part of a make-your-own gift set given to Anna for her birthday. She had thought her daughter hadn't even noticed it, so obsessed was the little girl with her Malibu Barbie beach hut. At some point over the last six months, however, Anna had snapped it together and decorated it with colourful sparkles and sequins. Encased within the cheap plastic frame was a photo of the four of them, taken last summer on their last holiday together in Lyme Regis. Adam, suntanned and smiling, was kneeling on the ground, arms around the children's waists, while Tess stood behind, both hands resting on his broad shoulders.

'We went fossil hunting,' whispered Anna. Tess looked up to see her daughter's eyes on her. 'Daddy and I. It was when you took Michael for his nap.'

'I remember.' Tess nodded. 'You both came back very pink and I was cross at Daddy for not putting sun cream on you.'

'I was only a little bit burned.'

'Yes.' Tess smiled. 'Only a little bit.'

'We looked and looked,' continued Anna, 'and when we couldn't find anything, Daddy took me to the shop and bought me a dinosaur's tooth.'

'A dinosaur's tooth!'

'Yep, one for me and one for him, a pair.' Anna smiled shyly and traced a small heart on the back of her mother's hand. 'He keeps his in his wallet for good luck, but I lost mine.'

'Ah.'

By now, Anna had edged her way across the bed towards her mother.

'Do you know,' said Tess, 'I still have Daddy's wallet at home.' She thought of the brown box, high on top of the wardrobe shelf. 'Instead of looking on the beach for one, maybe when we get home you and I can look through his things and find that special tooth.'

'I think that would be very nice, Mummy.'

Climbing in beside her, Tess snuggled in close and kissed her daughter's warm neck.

'I love you, Sweet Pea,' she whispered.

But the little girl was already fast asleep and dreaming.

The Rain in Spain

BY CATRIONA STEWART

*T*he plane drops out of the clouds into a sullen afternoon and touches down on a slick runway, rain slanting meanly against the porthole windows. Anne tries not to see, out of the corner of her eye, Jeremy's knuckles, white knots of tension across the top of his fists. He has no fear of flying or landing. She concentrates on the seat-belt sign and the conversation in the next row. A man's voice confidently predicts that the rain won't last. Anne checked the seven-day forecast online last night. He obviously hasn't. Or he wants to keep his wife upbeat about being on holiday. Like any half-decent husband.

Jeremy's pleasant to the shuttle-bus driver. She imagines him arranging his face back to the fixed expression he's adopted with her and avoids looking at him. As they leave the sprawling suburbs of Palma and head north, the rain develops into a full-blown thunderstorm, deep black clouds snagged on the jagged spine of the Sierra Montana. Anne watches for the next fork of lightning on the ridge, her view occasionally interrupted

293

by his reflection in the window. He's looking the other way. He would.

When they reach Puerto Pollensa, the driver mutters about the No Entry signs barring traffic from the beach area and drops them ungraciously in an alley near the back of the hotel. Anne leads the way through the puddles to the peeling stucco doorway. That didn't feature on the website. They're straight into a bar area with broken Roman columns and archways propped precariously against the walls. An Art Nouveau coat-stand, with hat-hooks shaped like overblown daisies, hovers in the middle of the archaeology. She stops herself shaking her head and glances at Jeremy. It's safe to assume she won't be allowed to forget she's booked this place.

At the reception desk, two grey-haired women with tight perms and flowery skirts discuss the weather with a receptionist called Amalia.

'Home from home,' says the first sister, leaning across the desk and pushing her glasses down her nose to read the computer screen.

'Look, it's warm,' says Amalia, 'with less precipitation later in the week. We've had no rain for months.'

'You need it, then,' confirms the other one, used to dispensing wisdom.

They stand there expectantly. Anne prepares for a long wait but Amalia turns and greets her warmly. Jeremy's wandered off to look through the front door at the sea and the old girls head in his direction, clutching their hardbacks. Anne pictures the size of their luggage. She's booked one of the most expensive rooms: sea view, balcony, bath and shower. The miraculous change out of Auntie Dennie's drinks money. She'd approve if she was still around.

'Jeremy, we're on the third floor.'

They face each other in the small lift. His eyes are raised to the ceiling. He must want to see where they're going this time. When they open the door to their room, it's dark and shuttered. Anne has imagined this bit, walking into a room flooded with afternoon sun, the sea glinting beyond the balcony doors, magically lifting the mood. She fiddles clumsily with the sliding door and opens the shutters. The cushions on the wicker chairs are soaking and a large succulent cactus with leaves like plump fingers oozes water extravagantly out of its terracotta pot.

The hotel sits in a huge crescent-shaped bay embraced by mountains. The sea is flat calm now the thunderstorm has moved away. Across the tops of feathery pine trees, a forest of dark masts in the marina stands out starkly against the pale-washed sky. Sleek sailing boats dot the bay randomly, showing up the sharp motor launches for uncouth gatecrashers. A solitary black cormorant moves across the marked-off swimming area, dives down and disappears in a shaft of weak sunlight. Anne wants to do the same.

Jeremy picks up the chair cushions and takes them to the bathroom, then consults his watch. It's after five o'clock, Spanish time.

'Let's go down and have a drink.'

He speaks.

Down at ground level, the sea is close, lapping the sand just beyond the terrace and the paired loungers under thatched umbrellas with their jaunty topknots. They find two dry chairs under an overhanging balcony and Jeremy orders a bottle of Majorcan rosé. Anne notes the compromise between his preference for red and hers for white. She grimly stirs a puddle next to her chair with one foot. It'll take more than that. The bottle arrives with green olives and bread. The waiter calls the wine 'fantastico', his long black curls bouncing around his shoulders. Anne is tempted to mention the weather to see what he'll say.

Jeremy refills their glasses quickly. Anne leans back, eyes shut, letting the sound and smell of the espresso machine, and the warmth from the bar behind them, wash over her. Within minutes, the rain is back, pock-marking the sea again. People flip-slop past with towels over their shoulders, breaking into a dash as the thunder reverberates across the bay. Water sluices off the huge parasols, pooling on tables. Mr Fantastico comes out to rescue menus and ashtrays, a white linen napkin draped over his head. Jeremy suppresses a smile and grabs the wine bottle.

'I'm getting wet.'

He speaks. Again.

Later, they find a pizzeria recommended by Amalia, under a huge awning on the seafront. They're just in time to get a small table on the edge before a wave of customers pile in. Jeremy's sunk into another silence.

The owner tells them which pasta has been freshly made that afternoon and recommends the red from Binissalem. Anne orders it, wondering whether she's throwing Jeremy's olive branch back in his face. In minutes, the waiter lights their candle and pours the wine, which splashes densely into her glass to try first. She looks across at Jeremy as she tastes it. He looks back, his face slightly animated at the prospect of more wine. She nods appreciatively and smiles up at the owner.

'Delicious, thank you.'

Jeremy picks up his glass and takes a small sip. 'Not bad.'

His courgette and mozzarella starter arrives quickly. Anne nurses her wine. He washes his food down, generously. Go on, she thinks, get drunk. The rain has stopped again and the marina lights spill like orange ribbons across the bay. Jeremy orders a second bottle and raises his glass to her. By the time the orange crème caramels arrive, she feels ready to burst, with food and everything else. The busyness of the place covers their silence.

She was so sure the sun always shone here. She wonders how they'll cope with a week of rain. The only formula is to keep drinking, buy more books. The sun was to shine hot on the damage they'd done to each other since he was made redundant.

Back at the hotel, they tumble on to the hard mattress and sleep restlessly. At one point, she hears him orienting himself in the dark, wrestling with the balcony door; he's fuddled, thinks he's at home.

In the morning, he's gone. She opens the shutters, hoping for a miracle. The scene is limpid. It's raining softly. There's no sign of him downstairs. The coffee from the self-service machine is tasteless, the croissant flabby. None of this would matter if the sun would only shine. She waits for him upstairs, trying to read, then goes down to the bar for a real coffee, and finally heads out into the rain. He's deliberately making her worry, disappearing like this. She forces herself not to look for him, eating tapas on her own in a back street. Later she walks for miles around the bay. He's in the bath when she gets back, his wet clothes draped over the chairs. At least she wasn't there when he came back.

He says nothing about where he's been but he looks fresh and taut. They find a restaurant Amalia says is famed for its local dishes. The food is good, an easy talking point. They drink only one bottle of wine and walk back under a full moon and stars.

Anne stops and looks up. 'Tomorrow might be better.'

'I enjoyed today.'

'Doing what?'

'Walking over to the other side of the peninsula. Good bird life.'

'You got drenched.'

He nods. 'The guy on reception's offered me an anorak next time.'

Anne thinks of her suggestion that he pack rain gear. She doesn't say it.

'I know. You told me. And I ignored you.'

He produces a bottle of Spanish brandy in their room.

'Want some?'

They sit on the balcony, watching the bay. Jeremy slaps a mosquito away and gets up to slide the balcony door shut. He pours a second glass, which they drink silently in the twinkling dark. The warmth from the alcohol doesn't last.

Anne gets up. 'It's getting chilly.' She searches for a handle on the door. 'You'll have to open it. I can't work out how to get in.'

Jeremy leans back and feels the door frame, then sits and looks at her.

'What?'

'Flaw in the design.'

'What do you mean?'

He starts to laugh.

'Bloody hell, J. Why did you shut it anyway?'

Tears run down his face. He's shaking with laughter. 'It's like us. Stuck out in the cold.'

Anne watches him sourly. 'It's not funny. You're drunk.'

'Lighten up, for pity's sake. It's a lot more fun than we've had for the last six months.'

She sits down again, arms wrapped round herself. 'Pour me another drink. And since you're having such fun, give me your jumper.'

The stars go out above them and it starts drizzling. Eventually the people next door appear on their balcony and let them in. Anne almost falls asleep in a hot bath, listening to Jeremy whistling tunelessly through his toothbrush.

The next morning, he's still in bed when she wakes. She knows without opening her eyes, feeling the heat come off him. She thinks about doing what he did yesterday and disappearing on her own for the day, but he reaches a hand out to her.

'Do you want to do that walk I did yesterday?'

She opens the shutters. 'It'll be in the rain.'

'Ah, but it's nice rain,' he says, jumping out of bed. 'I want to do it with a bird book this time.'

After breakfast, he goes off to find a bookshop while she waits for the espresso machine. He comes back with a book of walks in the Balearics and another about Mediterranean birds. He's like a man with a mission, partly accomplished. She remembers him when he was always like this, before being thrown off course. They kit up and set off across an urban park. He knows where he's going. Anne looks sideways at him, stirred by his purpose.

The rough stony track snakes uphill between limestone rocks. It's raining steadily. The sea and sky merge behind them and there's little to see through the mist ahead. Anne's soon cooking inside her anorak.

'God, I'm hot,' she mutters, stopping to take breath. She pushes her hood off. 'The jacket's not even waterproof.' She takes it off and ties it loosely round her waist. 'It's all right for you; yours is. I'll be eaten alive now.'

Jeremy pulls a spray out of his rucksack. 'Do you want some repellent?'

She reaches for it, not trusting herself to comment on his foresight.

'At least we've got the place to ourselves,' he says as they reach the top. 'Look. That bird climbing in tight circles. Must be a hoopoe. I was hoping to see one.'

He'd stopped hoping not long ago. He produces a bottle of water, takes a long slug and passes it to her.

She finishes half of it.

'I didn't think about water, with all this rain.'

They walk down a steep track in silence. There's a breeze now, clearing the mist so she can see down to a small cove. When her trainers lose traction near the bottom, she risks a big jump onto the crunchy shingle. They stand together looking at the silvery-green water. It's so clear you can see the sandy bottom and where the seaweed starts.

Anne sits down on the pebbles, wriggling her bum in, and unties her laces. She gets up again and peels off her wet jeans.

Jeremy watches her. 'Don't stop.'

'I'm not.' She gets down to bra and pants.

'Let me help.' He runs his hands down her back and undoes the hooks, slipping his fingers under the damp straps. She pulls away and kicks off her pants.

Like this, the breeze feels too cool. She doesn't wait, running towards the water and throwing herself in as soon as she feels it reach her waist. She wants to get past the uncertainty so it's only cold for a moment. She turns over, pushing away from the shore, looking back. Jeremy is naked, running in after her. He stands for a moment as the waves rise around him.

'He who hesitates is lost,' she calls.

'I've worked that out,' he shouts back.

He surfaces next to her, treading water, shaking himself like a dog.

'You need a haircut,' Anne tells him, staying low in the water to keep warm. His throat looks oddly vulnerable and she thinks she can hear the thump of his heart.

'Too shaggy? Am I?'

He pushes his thick hair back off his forehead. She floats away from him with her eyes shut. He won't see the tears mingle with the rain and the sea, salt running into salt. She feels his hand on her stomach. It just lies there quietly, not going anywhere. She imagines that they can stay here, frozen in time, with this peace between them.

The Anniversary

BY ALISON WEIR

'Can't find anywhere suitable,' Beth sighed, scrolling down *Places to Stay in East Sussex*. 'A lot of these hotels don't have websites. I just don't want to take a chance. It is our anniversary, after all.'

Joe bent over her shoulder.

'That place looks nice,' he suggested, pointing to a stately Georgian pile done up as a hotel.

'Far too expensive,' Beth reproved.

'Fair enough,' Joe agreed placidly. 'I'd rather keep some money for the meal. That place there has a good restaurant, it says.'

'Nouvelle cuisine,' Beth sniffed. 'I looked up the menu.'

'I like that one,' Joe said. The photograph showed a pretty pub with hanging baskets.

'So do I, but it's only got a three-star rating. Wait – look at that!' She pointed to a picture of an ancient beamed inn. 'That's lovely!'

'Yes, but go back for me and look up the website for the other place first,' Joe urged. Beth clicked.

'Too dear for what it is,' she said. 'I'll go back to that

303

old inn.' She tapped at the keys, then tapped again. 'That's funny. It was on this page, I'm sure, below that one.'

'You've gone back too far,' Joe told her.

'No, it was here. It's just disappeared.'

'Perhaps they've taken it off because it's full.'

'Do they do things like that? Can they?' Beth was often confused by modern technology. Joe shrugged.

'OK,' he said decisively, 'here's the deal. We drive down to Sussex and take pot luck. When we see a place we like the look of, we can go and check it out before booking.'

Beth brightened. 'That's a great idea. We could go early, to allow ourselves plenty of time.'

Joe kissed her. 'Can't wait!' he muttered, nuzzling her ear.

They left the main road before Lewes and drove south across country towards Battle. It was a warm, drowsy, late-August day, and England was basking in sunshine, its landscape a tapestry of greens and vivid florals. By three o'clock, they had inspected and rejected three hotels, and were becoming the tiniest bit demoralised, for they had hoped to check in with time to spare to visit Battle Abbey and enjoy afternoon tea in a quaint little café nearby.

As luck would have it, they saw the sign just north of Battle. White wood, with black-painted letters. *The Fighting Man. First left. Historic Inn offering Good Food and Accommodation.* Slowing the car, Joe looked at Beth.

'Shall we try it?'

'Why not? It sounds lovely – but let's see!'

They turned left and drove down a shady lane until they saw a pub sign depicting King Harold pierced with an arrow through the eye. It stood on a well-kept green in front of a beautiful old timbered building with a brass-studded oak door and diamond-paned, mullioned windows glinting in the afternoon sunshine. Through a brick archway to the right, they could see chairs and tables in a sheltered walled garden.

'Wow!' Beth breathed. 'Isn't that the one we saw online? The one that disappeared?'

'I'm not sure, but I think we've hit the jackpot.' Joe smiled. 'Let's investigate.'

He parked in the deserted car park on the left. The sun was beating down, and the air seemed unusually heavy – and still. They walked to the door, which opened at a touch. It led into the bar, but instead of boasting the predictable horse brasses, ladder-back chairs and chalkboards typical of a country inn, it was smart with beige walls, sleek, dark wooden tables adorned only by large, unlit candles, and high-backed chairs upholstered in aubergine tweed. There were beams, but they looked modern. Blue LED lights illuminated the rows of bottles and glasses ranked behind the bar. The room was empty.

Joe leaned across the bar and called, 'Hello!'

'Look, here's a menu,' Beth said. 'Mmm, this looks good.'

There was a thudding as if somebody was running

down carpeted stairs, and a man in his thirties entered the bar from its far end. He had spiky, ruffled, short hair and an earring, and wore combat trousers and a white T-shirt. He appeared to be a little out of breath, but his smile was friendly.

'Good afternoon,' he welcomed them. 'Can I help you?'

'We were wondering if you have a double room free for tonight?' Beth enquired. Her eyes were drawn to some raw, red patches on the man's neck and arms. She looked away quickly. It was rude to stare.

'Of course,' he smiled. 'We have two. Would you like to see them?'

'Yes please,' Joe replied. Their host led them through a doorway and up a narrow, uneven staircase carpeted in soft beige. Upstairs, three doors led off the landing. One was closed.

'There's no one else staying, so you can take your pick,' the man told them.

He pushed open the nearest door, and again, Beth noticed the angry skin on his arms. Then her attention was distracted, for the room was delightful, painted in restful cream and furnished with a four-poster, tasteful antiques and good toiletries. Somebody had evidently taken a lot of trouble restoring this place. But there was a strange, sour scent in the room, and the bed looked as if it had been made in a hurry . . .

Beth wrinkled her nose and looked at Joe. He made a face.

'That's an odd smell,' he remarked.

'I can't smell anything,' their host said, looking puzzled.

Beth turned away and walked into the second room. It was done up in soft lilac tones and smelled of fresh lemons.

'I like this one,' she said happily. 'What do you charge?'

'Normally ninety, but you can have it for seventy-five, as it's just the one night.'

'Done!' agreed Joe.

'Pay me on the way out.' With a smile, he opened the shut door and quickly disappeared through it. As it closed behind him, a girl's giggle could be heard. Beth raised her eyebrows, and Joe grinned.

They unloaded their small case, then drove to Battle Abbey as planned, congratulating themselves on finding such a delightful place to stay.

'I'm surprised it's not on the Internet,' Beth said, as they stood on the ridge of Senlac, gazing down at the peaceful meadows where the Conqueror's Norman hordes had gained their bloody victory.

'Perhaps it's only recently opened. Be grateful it's not online – a place like that would be mobbed.'

'There was an odd smell in that first bedroom,' Beth said. 'Like charred wood – and something else that I couldn't identify. I couldn't wait to get out. Anyway, that menu looks delicious.'

When they got back to The Fighting Man, they bought some drinks and took them outside, enjoying

the mild breeze as the sun set in a fiery haze of glory.
When their glasses were empty, they rose and, by un-
spoken mutual consent, went upstairs, where they lay
down on the bed, luxuriating in crisp white sheets and
downy pillows – and in each other.

At seven-thirty, they showered in the black-tiled en
suite with its fluffy, snow-white towels, and dressed for
dinner. Before they went downstairs, Joe pressed a tiny
box into Beth's hand, and she found inside a delicate
gold heart pendant on the slenderest of chains.

'Happy anniversary, darling,' he said, taking her in
his arms once again and kissing her.

Their host was waiting to show them to an intimate
corner table near the open fireplace, which was filled
with fresh flowers. The candles had been lit, and the
lounge bar looked warm and inviting. But strangely,
there were still no other patrons in evidence.

'Where is everybody?' Beth wondered. 'A lovely
place like this . . .'

'Probably a lot of competition around here,' Joe
observed. 'Or the food's rubbish!'

'I hope not. You know, it's almost eerie. Not quite
right. I can't put my finger on it.'

'You're imagining it. I like the sense of peace here –
it's relaxing.' He winked at her.

'Is it normally this quiet?' he asked, as they ordered
the wine – a fruity Verdicchio.

'It's unusual for this time of year,' their host
shrugged, 'but it's a Monday night, of course. Come
the weekend . . .'

'Have you been open long?' Beth asked.

'My girlfriend and I bought the place just over a year ago,' he replied. 'The idea was to offer something different from the usual pub grub and "olde worlde" atmosphere. But it's been a struggle, I don't mind telling you. People around here don't go to pubs for fine dining. I wish we had more customers like you! Now, are you ready to order?'

The stuffed mushrooms were delicious, and the blackened Cajun salmon that followed was a dish to die for. As for the brandy syllabub . . .

'That was superb,' Joe said, folding his napkin.

'We must come here again,' Beth enthused.

Their host took their plates and their order for coffee, then came back with two small schooners of limoncello.

'On the house.' He beamed.

Back in bed, beneath the waffled cream blankets, Beth and Joe lay replete with good food and wine. Just as Beth felt a great tide of desire, Joe reached for her ardently. God, she thought, some while later, it hasn't been this good in years! What's got into us? In fact, it hadn't been that good ever. It was almost as if they had been taken over by something that was no part of either of them. Could this place have something to do with it? As dawn broke, however, she dismissed this idea as pure imagination. 'It must have been the wine,' she told herself, smiling.

*

After a hearty late breakfast, served at the same table, but this time with the sunlight flooding through the ancient windows, they paid their bill.

'Do come again,' the proprietor said. 'It's been a pleasure to have you.'

'We certainly will,' they said, and thanked him, then went to collect their case from the room.

'Just leave the keys on the bar on your way out.'

They did just that, along with a ten-pound note in recognition of his warm and friendly service.

They were in no hurry to return to London, so spent the day in Hastings, wandering around the castle and the caves, and enjoying fish and chips at a little seafront restaurant in the Old Town. They were still singing the praises of The Fighting Man, and when it came to the time to drive home, Beth was thoughtful.

'Joe, are you in any hurry to get back tonight?'

'No. I've brought some manuscripts home to read. I wasn't planning to go back to work until Friday. Why?'

'Well, I thought we could go back to that place for one more night. It was so lovely. And I don't have any appointments tomorrow.' Beth was a speech therapist, with her own private practice.

Joe looked at her delightedly.

'Why not?'

They drove back to Battle, dusk settling around them, until the trees were black silhouettes against the red-gold sky. North of the town they took the road that led the way they had come the previous day, and watched out for the white sign.

'I'm sure it was closer to Battle than this,' Joe puzzled, after they had driven about three miles and it was growing quite dark.

'Perhaps we missed it.'

'I'll turn round and go back,' Joe said, but they still did not see the sign.

They stopped at a garage to get petrol and buy water.

'We're trying to find a pub called The Fighting Man,' Joe told the plump lady who was swiping his credit card. 'Do you know it?'

'I did,' she said.

'Did?' Beth asked, startled at her use of the past tense.

'Nice place it was. And the couple that bought it spent a lot doing it up.'

'Was?' Joe echoed.

'All gone now,' the woman went on. 'They're still sorting out the insurance, I heard. There wasn't a will, you see. It was all in the local paper.'

'Gone?'

'Burned down a year ago this month. Terrible tragedy. Those poor souls. They were ever such a happy couple.' She leaned forward. 'Faulty wiring. It was the middle of the day. Found them in the bedroom, you know. In that four-poster bed.' She gave them a knowing look and shook her head sadly.

'Burned down?' Beth cried. 'It can't have. We stayed there last night!'

'That must have been somewhere else,' the woman said.

'Yes,' Joe put in, folding an arm round Beth and steering her towards the door. He was trembling. 'We must have got it wrong. Sorry to have troubled you.'

When they got outside, Beth was shaking too. The raw patches – the burns – on the man's skin; that smell of scorched wood; the silence; the emptiness; the giggling girl hiding upstairs, waiting to return with her lover to that terrible room, on this first anniversary . . . and that inexplicable burst of passion. They were all starting to make bizarre, horrible sense . . .

'This is crazy!' Beth wailed. 'She must have been wrong.'

'Wait!' Joe fumbled in his shoulder bag. 'Look! The credit card receipt. It says The Fighting Man, Northiam Lane, by Battle. Come on, we'll find someone else to ask.'

As they drove back towards Battle, they passed an AA man, sitting astride his motorbike in a lay-by, drinking coffee.

'Excuse me, do you know Northiam Lane?' Beth called.

'Keep going, it's next on the right,' the AA man replied.

It was, but there was no sign that they could see, and the road was well-lit.

'That's odd,' muttered Joe. Beth shivered. Suddenly,

she didn't want them to drive down that lane, didn't want to discover what lay at the end of it. But Joe was accelerating forward, his face set, as it always was when he was nervous and didn't want to show it.

There was no welcoming pub sign. Just a roofless ruin of blackened bricks, jagged timbers and rubbish. A makeshift barbed-wire fence had been erected around the site, with a notice saying 'Danger, Keep Out'. The whole place was repellent, sinister. Where only last night there had been warm lights and laughter, there was now just a tragic silence and the dark, windy sky.

Joe moved forward, flashing the torch he always kept in his pocket for emergencies.

'No!' Beth cried, her instincts telling her to run.

But Joe had seen something.

There was no door, although its frame remained. A little way inside lay what was left of the bar. There was something on the floor. His feet crunched over the ash and the rubble.

'Joe, be careful!' Beth warned. But Joe did not heed her. He bent down and picked up something, then something else. Then he turned to face her and held out his hand. His face was shadowed in the torchlight, but she could sense the tension in him.

'We were here,' he faltered, his voice unsteady. 'Look. The keys. And my ten-pound note.' They lay there in his trembling palm.

The Best Little Book Club in Town

Contributors' copyright information:

breast
cancer
care

Breast Cancer Care is here for anyone affected by
breast cancer. We bring people together, provide
information and support, and campaign for improved
standards of care. We use our understanding of
people's experience of breast cancer and our clinical
expertise in everything we do.

Every year more and more people need our support.
By buying this book, you are helping us to be there for
every one of them. We are also enormously grateful to
Orion Books and *woman&home* for their generous
support in bringing this book to you.

If you would like more information about our work,
you can visit www.breastcancercare.org.uk or call our
free helpline on 0808 800 6000.